Lanchester Library

WITHDRAWN

D1630173

**British Design & Art Direction
in collaboration with
Rotovision SA**

RotoVision

the product book

£37-50

Acknowledgments

Book Design
Kate Stephens

Cover Illustration
George Hardie

Editor
Catherine McDermott

Managing Editor
Marcelle Johnson

Project Manager
John Green

**D&AD would like to thank British Steel
and the Design Council for their
support for The Product Book.**

British Steel

**We would also like to thank all the contributors
who so generously gave their time for this book.**

Published by RotoVision SA
Rue du Bugnon 7
CH-1299 Crans-Près-Céligny
Switzerland

RotoVision SA, Sales & Production Office
Sheridan House, 112/116A Western Road
Hove, East Sussex BN3 1DD, UK

Tel: +44 (0) 1273 72 72 68
Fax: +44 (0) 1273 72 72 69
e-mail: sales@RotoVision.com

First published 1999
Copyright © British Design & Art Direction 1999
A D&AD Mastercraft Series publication

Production and Separation in Singapore
by ProVision Pte Ltd
Tel: +65 334 7720
Fax: +65 334 7721

Printed in Singapore. All rights reserved.
Without limiting the rights under copyright above, no part of
the publication may be reproduced, stored in or introduced into
a retrieval system, or transmitted, in any form or by any means
(electronic, mechanical, photocopying, recording or otherwise),
without the prior written permission of both the copyright
owner and the above publisher of this book.

ISBN No. 2–88046–394–7

Contents

Introduction

Catherine McDermott

The twentieth century is a world of transformations where instantaneous, electronic communication has changed the quality of our everyday experience forever. Within this world product design has influenced lives in a truly global sense. It is the interface with the communication revolution of radios, televisions, mobile phones and computers. Product design is not only about defining the present but also the future. Its mindset is fixed to gaze years ahead, to the point at which some designers claim not only to predict the future, but also to actually "do" the future. As consumers we have come to expect product designers to create magic on a regular and repeated basis.

Product design has shaped the unique culture of the twentieth century. Products signal fundamental change and become the visible signs of cultural shifts. Products, for example, used to identify nations. Increasingly, however, these boundaries of national identity have become blurred. In the new techno-world, the product designer is a nomad in the global marketplace. Nations, as the Japanese writer Kenneth Ohmae pointed out, have now become mere fictions[1]. They have been replaced by new economic and cultural zones such as Silicon Valley, represented here by Jonathan Ive of Apple, Steve Peart of Vent and Bill Moggridge of IDEO; all are Brits relocated to California.

New meanings have developed within the territory of consumption. In the early decades of the twentieth century production was the important focus, now consumption is the nexus of discussion. The relationship between the user's needs and desires and the object are at the heart of our experience of the world. The designer remains a key player but we are all included in the team as consumers, producers and silent designers shaping our experience of the world. Products now claim the clear message that design is not a lifestyle issue but a force for change and a way to enhance industrial performance and prosperity.

At the end of the twentieth century product design has broadened in scope to incorporate strategic consulting in brand development. Companies have learnt to speak through advertising and branding as well as their products and it has been called 'convergence' where product design becomes the old style brand message and products combine both the media and the technology. Product design and advertising share an intellectual process, both communicate the identity, quality, function and significance of the object. Both employ a common visual vocabulary and combine to make it work better. The Apple iMac and its integration of object with copy and advertising image is such an example. In the 1990s both advertising and design form the basis of the creative industries.

The Product Book is the fourth title in the D&AD Mastercraft series in which 29 of the world's directional design companies introduce their current work and aspirations. *The Product Book* invited each designer or team member to talk directly to the reader and to address issues such as the organisation of the studio, key projects, their relationship with both client and consumer and strategies concerning the future. The selection is international and put together by an advisory panel including the Museum of Modern Art in New York and San Francisco and the Victoria and Albert Museum in London. In this way *The Product Book* documents important change, providing the reader with a unique map surveying the product design profession and its agenda at the end of the century.

The individual entries in the book reveal histories and futures. Some product design pioneers of the twentieth century have survived. In 1991, the Dutch company Philips celebrated 100 years of creative work, signalling a tradition of manufacturers who have held out for quality and innovation. Raymond Loewy's 1930s blueprint for a design office lives on in third generation practices such as Seymour Powell, Hollington, James Irvine, Ross Lovegrove and Sowden Associates. Close on their heels is a fourth generation of design offices, including Lunar, tangerine and TKO. The size and nature of these 29 design companies are diverse. Some are internationally-known manufacturing companies with an in-house design team, such as Apple, Philips, Renault and Dyson. Some have multiple-location offices offering the client a portfolio of specialist services, such as IDEO, Pentagram and frog. Others such as Sebastian Bergne and StudioBrown are small, individual offices. They are consistent in the importance they place on teamwork and their ambitions for a close and seamless relationship with industry. Teamwork however is not the most important issue for another group of designers. Marc Newson, Jasper Morrison, Ron Arad and Karim Rashid, for example, are not immediately identifiable as traditional "product designers". Their work suggests a parallel theme within the product design, the individual creative, offering the manufacturer a vision which gives the product their identifiable signature and aesthetic.

By offering such a diversity of approach *The Product Book*'s essays make for fascinating reading. They are inward and outward reflections on the product design profession and the future. At the end of the 1990s they define ideas of best practice, the interaction with technology, old and new relationships with manufacturing industry and the morality of producing more and more 'stuff'. Other issues rooted in the reformist tradition of the nineteenth century are firmly back on the agenda. The talk is of morality in design and a duty to make things better for people – access to design for all. At one end of the design spectrum these themes are reflected in the work of Tucker Viemeister for utensils for people with a wide range of abilities and at the other, the young JAM team. The moral obligation of the designer to consider the long-term impact of work has become more than a matter of personal choice. Projected global population figures suggest a population rise to around twelve billion against a current figure of around six billion. Meeting these needs will be the basis for a sustainable future and the need for 'joined-up thinking' to interact with all aspects of design. Sustainable product design in which designers face the challenge of creating goods that consume less energy and can be recycled at the end of their lives is vital to cutting environmental pollution. Designers have to secure economic and constructive solutions to these problems.

As we leave the twentieth century we believe that *The Product Book* is a unique publication that audits the concerns and challenges facing not only designers but also manufacturers and consumers. It is an opportunity for us to take stock and for future generations to judge a material culture that reflects our values, our aspirations and our creativity.

More than ever before, industry needs design. British manufacturing and British culture underestimate product design. Compared with Information Technology, product design has only a modest prominence in the media. Indeed, product design and steel have both become such a normal part of life that they are, today, rather taken for granted. But this situation is poised to change. In their search to stand out from the crowd, more and more giant corporations will come to see product design as a key source of competitive differentiation and added value. They will realise what we at British Steel have long known: good product design is crucial to commercial success.

Steel is used in many sectors, from airports and cars to packaging and jewellery. Whatever part is required, we are able to tailor a selected steel for the particular needs. However, we also know that without the creative influence of the designer, the visual and tactile possibilities in steel and its capacity to delight will not be evident. To deliver real innovations to the market, industry has to offer technical support to designers. Designers may not be our direct customers, but they are the people who make innovations happen.

Of course, designers need industry. That is why British Steel is pleased to sponsor this book on their behalf as part of our work with D&AD. We have a responsibility to ensure that steel plays a full part in realising the potential of product design to change the world around us. Yet we support *The Product Book* for reasons wider than this.

First, the skills used for good design, and design itself, have grown more sophisticated. Objects made from steel can be stronger, lighter, faster and cheaper to make, easier to transport and install. Steel is endlessly recyclable. The design process can benefit from the use of computer systems. Perhaps most significantly, designers now consider not just the physical artefact, but also the user's experience of the service that nowadays tends to accompany that artefact.

This widening of the product designer's role to include the interface and experience that a complete product-and-service system presents to users, is something we know and care a lot about at British Steel. A large part of the value we add for our customers lies not in the physical material we produce, but rather in the service that goes with it. Some of that service is about making the purchase and delivery of steel easier for our customers and for designers. Much, however, is also about British Steel providing the very best expertise about how to work in steel.

That brings me to the second reason why we are so enthusiastic about *The Product Book*. It reinforces a lesson we have learnt through the success of our services – that innovation is as much about the contribution made by people as it is about technology.

Seventy per cent of the steels we sell today have been developed in the past decade. Our people listen, early on, to what the customer wants to achieve with steel in terms of performance. They listen, too, to what the customer feels will be the likely pattern of future demand for steel.

This work of listening is only the starting point for creative innovation, but it is one that our people share with designers. The innovations covered in this book cannot be reduced to technique, but begin with a sensitivity to customers that is very human.

In turn, that enables me to conclude with the third and perhaps most central reason why *The Product Book* is so important for us. We want to celebrate the new, more sophisticated product design because of its relevance to management and industry in the new millennium.

Product design embraces users' needs and the tactile texture of day-to-day life. It is about listening to users, representing their interests and identifying those needs and wants which they may only be aware of subconsciously. Product design conveys the tone of voice in which a manufacturer wants to conduct a dialogue with the user. It communicates the company's values and its brand, since it guides the interactions that the user has with the product.

For all these reasons, product design has elements that go beyond the artefacts it directly develops. In its orientation toward users and what matters to them, product design provides a style of thinking which every kind of manager can benefit from.

At British Steel a key part of reinventing a 40,000-employee, seven-billion-pound-turnover company comes by concentrating upon steel's applications and its performance. That means that, through our everyday work, we are continually finding out the answers to that classic and, for us, perennial question of marketing: "What business are you in?" In many ways, the internationally acclaimed designers profiled in this book are excellent interpreters of what business their clients are in.

By emulating product designers' ceaseless efforts to discover and unlock all the user benefits latent within a product, manufacturers and service organisations will draw closer to the stated and unstated wants of their customers. That will help them to enter the new century with innovations every bit as exciting as those that are illustrated in this book.

The Design Council Perspective
John Sorrell, Chairman, Design Council

The Design Council shares a very simple, very ambitious goal with every single product designer in this book – to improve our quality of life. And looking through these pages, it is crystal clear why product design and quality of life go hand-in-hand.

What other discipline has so much potential to change our lives? In what other field can the designer do so much to transform the way we interact with the world around us? The way we see it, hear it, feel it, taste it?

Uniquely, product design has the ability to do all this and, at its best, change the way we lead our lives.

A good product has a major impact on how we work, on our efficiency and our effectiveness. It transforms the way we learn, opening up new modes of communication and new interfaces with new realms of knowledge. It also transforms the way we relax, improving and enhancing our ability to rest and recharge.

Truly well-designed products not only work their magic through the achievements of the individual, however. The really good product has an effect which reaches as far as an organisation is prepared to take it. At its most powerful, this impact can be dramatic. Not just for profits or the bottom line, nor even in reversing long periods of decline, although all these are possible, often with products which do not at first seem destined for significant success.

A really successful product can perform astonishing feats for profile, reputation and morale, too. It can foster ownership of a brand, reinforce buy-in, mend corporate damage and create tidal waves of publicity. It can rejuvenate tired images, create a new sense of pride and give new direction to previously empty, uncertain strategies. Beyond this, the successfully designed product becomes, by its very nature, a powerful vehicle with which companies can move with confidence into an increasingly demanding future. A future where information will be even more accessible, more quickly, than it is now, where technology will develop even faster and science will open up ever more extraordinary horizons. A future where the limits of our capabilities are only confined by the limits of our imagination.

It is only the most creative, most questioning and most imaginative mindsets which will be able to exploit this brave new world. The kind of mindsets which have produced the quite brilliant work which you will find in these pages. The dawn of the new millennium is a wholly appropriate time to publish such a stunning collection. Indeed, some of the work shown here has already achieved Millennium Product status, having been selected by the Design Council as being particularly innovative, ground-breaking and challenging. And it is through collections of work like these that others may find the inspiration needed to make the leap into the excitement and uncertainty of new product creation.

But perhaps the unsung hero of this book is the client, the customer, the commissioning company. For even the most talented product designer can be hamstrung by over-cautiousness or absence of vision from the host organisation. And yet consider the leaps of faith made on these pages by companies which, at a time of ever fiercer markets and intensive global competition, had the courage to invest in a mere germ of an idea, without knowing whether that investment would succeed.

The companies which have that courage and the vision to work with brilliant designers to create great products can, as this book shows, truly change the way we lead our lives.

   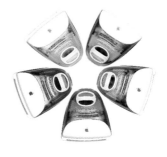

   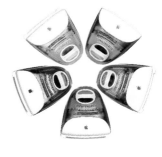

apple

Apple Computer Inc

Jonathan Ive

A good idea can circumnavigate the distractions and rhetoric that exist at the periphery of our profession. This truth haunts me, reminding me how much time I have wasted.

Wrestling with the real issues so often falls casualty to the inordinate amount of time designers spend justifying the value of their work, articulating their difference or competing for commissions. Justification rather than exploration.

Initially I believed that Apple offered an environment in which I could focus solely on design. Unfortunately I was horribly wrong. It was not until Steve Jobs returned to the company that I found myself in a precious and privileged situation; being part of a design team encouraged and supported in the pursuit of nothing other than good design.

Formerly, while consulting in London, I found myself working on programmes that posed distinct and polar problems. For Ideal Standard I designed washbasins and toilets in ceramic. The object's form and function were so closely coupled they defined the product's meaning and identity. While this presented very direct challenges I became increasingly interested in the opportunity to define an object's identity based upon a less obviously prescribed proposition.

Consulting for Apple, designing products whose essential function remains a total mystery to most of us, I was struck by the immense opportunity that existed to create new objects whose identity had previously been configured arbitrarily. Even the word "computer" had come to mean everything and nothing. Significantly impacting such a successful and wildly pervasive product category, and by implication millions of users, presented a particularly rare opportunity.

While these were compelling issues to explore I became increasingly frustrated that few ideas were ever realised. Models and prototypes became nothing more than the conclusions to a particular thought. They got dusty and only a handful of people ever saw them. Terrified that I was unable to have anything other than a fairly superficial impact as an external consultant I accepted a position at Apple.

We have assembled a heavenly design team. Keeping the core team small, by investing significantly in tools and process, allows us to work with a level of collaboration that seems particularly rare. Our physical environment reflects and enables our approach. The large open studio and massive sound system support a number of communal design areas. We have little exclusively personal space. In fact, the memory of how we work will endure beyond the products of our work.

Beyond the team – our work and process – the realisation that our effectiveness is primarily defined by our context within the larger company has been humbling. We are particularly conscious that we exist in an environment and at a point in time where we have the opportunity to focus exclusively on design and enjoy the support necessary to turn fragile ideas into reality. Value can be significant even if its measures are neither empirical nor easy to articulate. So often as designers we deny this by our preoccupation with justification. The obsession in the computer industry with microprocessor speed or hard drive capacity has reduced the conversation to the proposition of five being greater than two. Countless industries bear witness to this creative bankruptcy as attributes that are more difficult to comprehend and certainly more difficult to quantify are ordinarily ignored.

Ironically, these product attributes are often undermined by tools that have been developed to help evaluate and articulate value. One that I find particularly infuriating is the focus group. Viewed as a safer or more substantial alternative to 'the big idea' they can dilute intent and ultimately threaten innovation. Not for one moment am I advocating any detachment from customers. On the contrary, we spend a considerable amount of time with our customers to help construct our goals and inform our thinking, but trying to make decisions or evaluate ideas that are intended for tomorrow poses complex problems from the context of today. Essentially, vision describes not only a founding idea but necessarily the resolution to ensure its realisation.

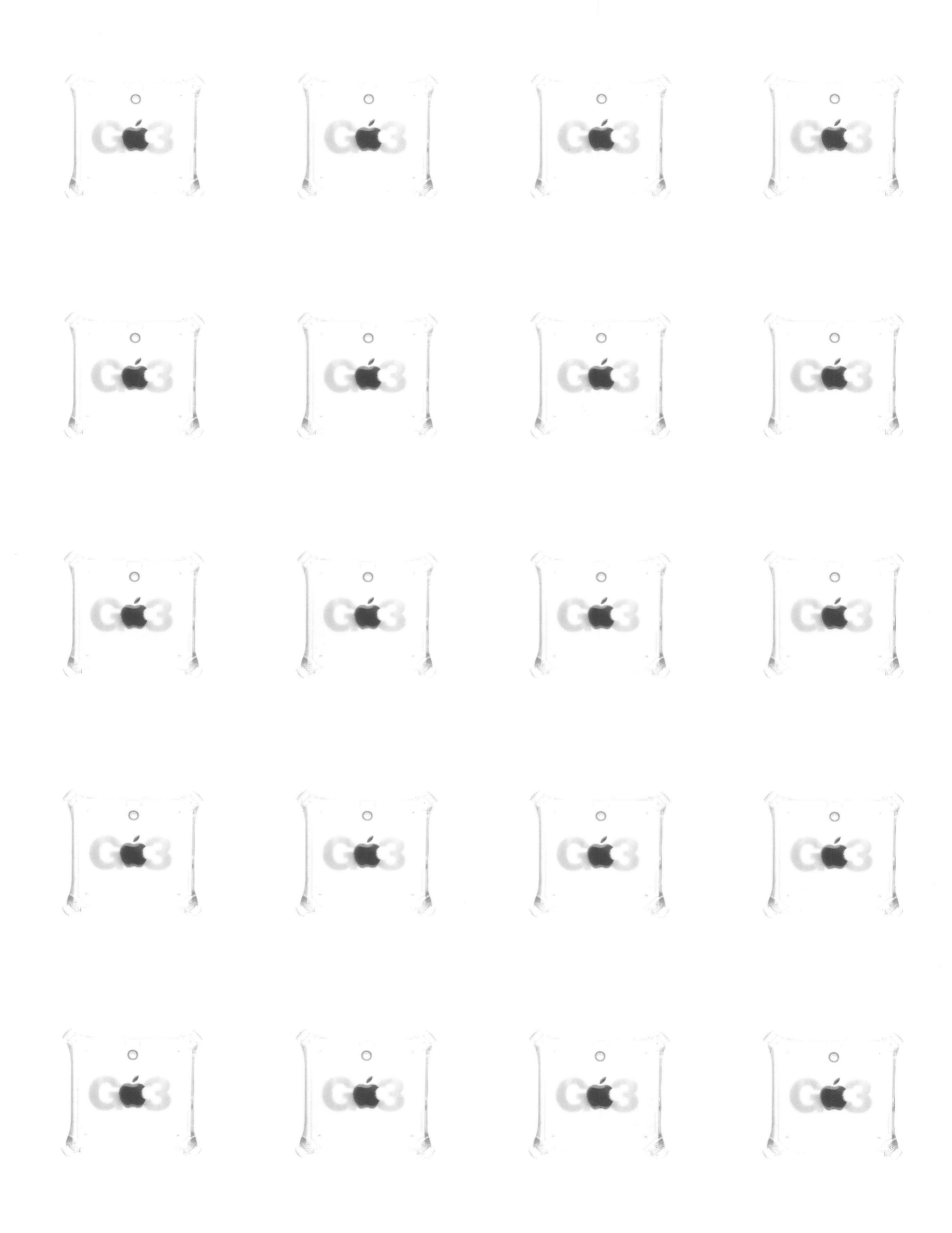

The animated and vital reaction to the iMac seems to have transcended geographic boundaries. One primary objective for the design of the iMac was to create something accessible, understandable, almost familiar. Creating something known clearly presents little challenge but trying to combine the familiar with the new, with something from tomorrow was more problematic. This paradox represented a particularly fertile point of departure. While I do not like the 'retrofuturist' tag, it is in some senses an affirmation that we went some way to achieving our goals.

Our attempts to make iMac less exclusive and more accessible occurred at a number of different levels. A detail example is the handle. While its primary function is obviously associated with making the product easy to move, a compelling part of its function is the immediate connection it makes with the user by unambiguously referencing the hand. That reference represents, at some level, an understanding beyond even the product's core function. Seeing an object with a handle, you instantly understand aspects of its physical nature – I can touch it, move it, it's not too precious...

While we were preoccupied with creating a more accessible, more democratic product we also invested considerable effort in trying to configure its identity appropriately. Constructing a narrative relative to core functionality prompted our intrigue with the chameleon-like nature of its function. One minute it's a writing machine, the next a video editing machine. This describes a fundamental and almost unique capability. While elsewhere great energy is being spent creating singular function appliances we wanted to celebrate this spectacular ability of the object to transform. The properties of the translucent material, shifting the emphasis from surface to light helped define a fluid object.

Beyond our goals and varying levels of success what has been truly consequential has been witnessing the reaction to the product. People smile when they see an iMac.

Torso
Suspension/Table Lamp

Client
Proto Design

Distribution
Authentics, Artipresent
Gmbh
1997

Made from one piece of cast
ceramic, the three-ended
form makes it possible to use
as a suspension or table lamp
in different orientations.

bergne

Bergne: design for manufacture
Sebastian Bergne

Photograph: Sebastian Bergne

Ring

Soap & Peg

Client
Authentics, Artipresent
Gmbh
1994

A ring of natural glycerine
soap that is stored by hanging
on a plastic peg. The soap
always remains dry and
becomes a graphic element in
the bathroom or kitchen.

Sip

Tasting Spoon

Client
Authentics, Artipresent
Gmbh
1998

A tasting spoon that allows
you to cool hot soups or
sauces by passing them from
one bowl to the other before
drinking. Hygienic, heat
resistant polypropylene
avoids burnt lips or
background flavours.

For me the role of an industrial designer must be to solve problems and create mass-produced objects in a way that contributes positively to people's lives and in so doing becomes part of our culture. The way different designers approach this problem-solving activity makes industrial design a wonderful and diverse profession. There is always another valid way to design something. For me, a well-designed object is one that makes me smile when I see or use it. This might be because it surprises me, has character, triggers some kind of recognition, is the right price, or simply because it is an innovative solution to a problem.

I think the most important thing I ever learned was how to look. From my childhood exposure to foreign cultures to my everyday environment here in London, observing and extracting something of interest from the obvious or seemingly banal has always been crucial in my work. Taking everyday life and what already exists as a starting point to what could or should exist has become the key to the way I approach my work today. This is in effect a pursuit of innovation in a broad sense of the word through a combination of cultural reference, humour, functional re-evaluation, and a close contact with materials and manufacturing technology. Each project is a new beginning...

The fact that my education could be described as a formal industrial design training means that there is a potential anomaly between the way that I work and the traditions of the field I am in. Having a personal approach to designing mass-produced products could create problems when designing products for manufacturers who want you to design something to fit a corporate vision that you don't necessarily agree with. In reality, the situation is that rather than changing how I design to fit a given client's idea of what they need, whatever the product area, I need to find clients who want to work with me because of the way that I approach the design process.

Photograph (Prototype) Sebastian Bergne / Bergne: design for manufacture

IXIX table

Client
Vitra Gmbh
1998

There was no formal briefing at the start of the project, but it soon defined itself as a single trestle table where the top would automatically attach to the structure without locks or catches. My primary historical reference was a traditional butler's tray and stand. It needed to be that easy to set up and put away. Achieving the final design took about two years with most of the work done in a series of mock-ups and prototypes (the first shown here). The project solution relies on the scissor action of the legs. It is the downward pressure of the top that pushes the legs apart and so locks the table more and more firmly onto the legs. Conversely, in order to separate the parts, lifting the top relieves the pressure and releases the top. The top can simply be put on and taken off, with a solid lock between the parts when they are in use.

Lamp Shade

Client
Radius Gmbh
1991

Having found an interesting material and manufacturing process (acid etching) that needed very low tooling investment and could be produced at a reasonable price, my goal became to solve the problem of the ubiquitous hanging light bulb. My solution shades and directs the light as an up or downlighter but does not hide the functional beauty of the bulb. The design relies on the bulb visually in its composition, and physically to keep the sprung stainless steel in its sinuous form. After producing and selling the lamp in small quantities myself, it generated enough interest to lead to the German manufacturer Radius Gmbh taking over first its distribution and then its full-scale manufacture.

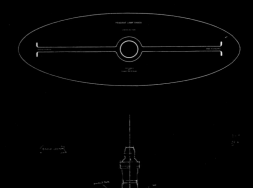

Leg Over

Stool

Client

Authentics, Artipresent Gmbh
1998

Leg Over is a stacking stool
that can be assembled with
one wing nut and a clip on top.
The traditional construction
has been quietly redefined by
the intelligent use of the
structural and visual qualities
of translucent polypropylene.

Mr Mause
Clothes Hanger
Client
D-House, Driade spa
1996

A clothes hanger that uses bottle brush technology to effectively pad hanging garments. Mr Mause is at the same time a functional innovation and a visual pun.

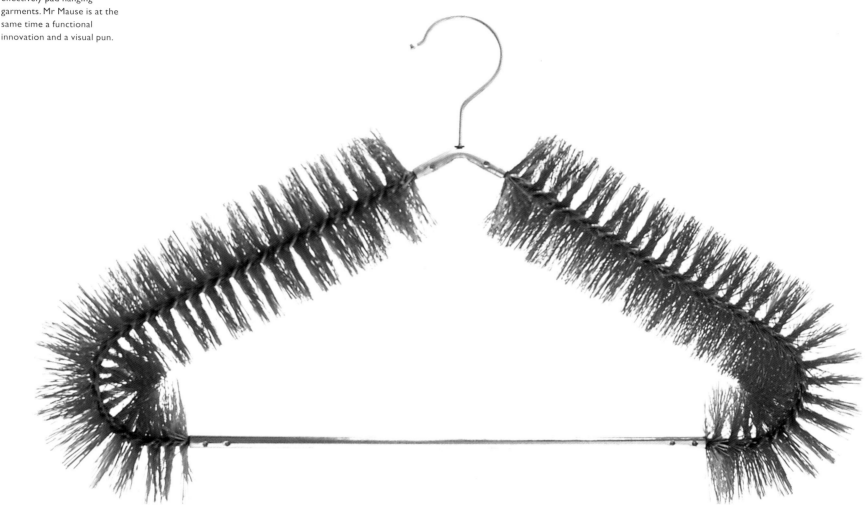

It is clear that my relationship with a client is extremely important. I prefer to have fewer long-standing clients than many shorter-term relationships. I strongly feel that it is only by working together over a period of time that you really begin to be a true partner in the process of developing the right new products for a given company. This of course means that it really needs to be me personally who is designing the product and that the person I am talking to in the manufacturing company is ideally the person who can make the final decision whether to go ahead with a project.

The effect of my client relationships on the size of my studio and way of working is profound. When I work on a project, the client is interested in me being personally involved in all stages of the design process, from concept to implementation. This means that I cannot delegate whole projects within my studio, limiting how many different projects I can take on at the same time. The design assistants that I work with take on a great deal of the "process" work, and give an important other view point, but it is important to me to be very involved in all aspects of the process. A limit in quantity of projects running concurrently does not limit the size of the projects, and in the end is very much to my advantage. The whole process is less about maintaining a high turnover of work to cover overheads and more about being happy with the quality and consistency of the projects leaving the studio.

My plans for the future depend very much on developing existing and creating new, lasting client relationships in different areas of mass-produced products. The design of electronic products is an area with ever-increasing potential, and one of which I have only scratched the surface. To design for public spaces has been a desire for some time and, since becoming a father, I have become increasingly aware of the possibilities in baby and children's products. Above all however, I hope that the future will allow me to continue working in a field where the work is always refreshing and never done.

donegani & lauda

Donegani & Lauda

Dante Donegani and Giovanni Lauda

Passepartout

Chaise Longue

Design
Dante Donegani, Giovanni Lauda

Client/manufacturer
Edra
1998

Carved out of a soft polyurethane
(with a metal structure) Passepartout
is a void shaped as a chaise longue,
a frame that cuts whole chunks out
of a space. The overall dimensions are
those of a normal chaise longue but
it differs because of its vertical
expansion. Passepartout is a tessera
in a larger mosaic of thoughts on
the dwelling ethic put together on
the 25th anniversary of "Italy: the
new domestic landscape", the
exhibition staged at MOMA in
New York in 1972.

We work together as a team in Milan. Our university studies, carried out respectively in Florence and Naples, had pushed us to Milan in search of greater creative freedom. The lessons we learnt from the masters of the "New Italian Design" were not only concerned with typological and linguistic innovations but also towards greater theoretical and professional rigour directed towards design. In the 80s, Milan was for us the centre of design along with Memphis, Alchimia, "Domus" magazine and the Domus Academy. It was in fact at the Domus Academy, a postgraduate school in Milan, where we met.

The tradition that we became part of, as architects and designers, was the typical non-specialisation of the Italian approach. That approach ranges from product to interiors and architecture, and gives particular attention to the physical and theoretical context of products, and consequently to the relationship between objects and space. Our first collaborations with professional studios and Milanese companies gave us the chance to understand the complexity of the theoretical, technical, and strategic problems confronted in the elaboration of a product: from the concept to its development and communication. After opening our own studio and deciding to work together, we have also explored many different sectors both as business professionals and as researchers: including product design and furniture, architectural competitions, interior design, equipment for art exhibitions, stands for fairs and education.

This continuous exercise of project gymnastics is very useful because it constantly modifies our design perspective by transferring experiences from one field to another, and from one scale to another. Also our commitment to design means that we are continuously proposing new themes that help us reflect on the large transformations occurring in the home and the city. Commissioned work is often limited to interior design and furniture projects. We have never built architecture but we freely choose the competitions in which to participate. Our relationship with the design business is one of great independence. Sometimes a product can develop by chance; with an affinity of ideas, from an exhibition, a theoretical idea or from a publication.

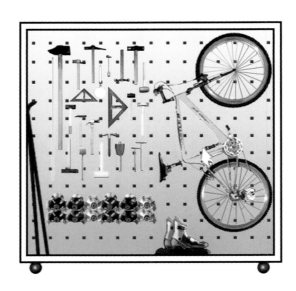
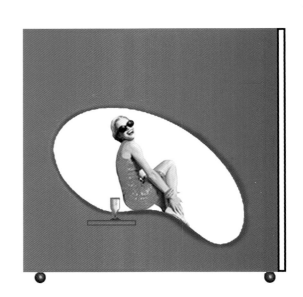

Disappearing Acts

Model Apartment

Design
Dante Donegani,
Giovanni Lauda, Jae Kyu Lee,
Elena Mattei
1997

In order to obtain greater
domestic mobility and
freedom, resources and
functions should be
combined. In this project,
domestic activities are
enclosed inside pull-out
components with standard
dimensions as "custom-made,
fully equipped boxes".
Empty space becomes a
source of pleasure. Furniture
disappears, reduced to
"negative" moulds or cavities
shaped to follow the forms of
their inhabitants. Elsewhere
objects are integrated by
electrical appliances in
vanishing wall closets.
Nature, enclosed and
compacted (greenhouse,
aviary, aquarium) becomes
an environmental tent, an
artificial landscape that
mediates between home
and city.

25

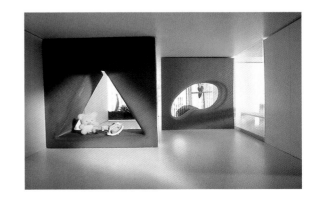

Quant
Office System

Design
Dante Donegani,
Giovanni Lauda

Client/manufacturer
Radice
1996

An office system suitable for home work – shelves, bookcases and cabinets are mounted on the same metal structure. The names derives from Mary Quant, the inventor of the mini-skirt, and refers to the 'skirt' that functions as a modesty panel or, when folded back and hooked to the structure, becomes a channel for wiring. The other accessories – the support for the CPU, the felt pocket for stationery, the drawer unit – are also suspended from the tubular structure.

**Compact
(Mini, Midi, Maxi)**
Workstations

Design
Dante Donegani,
Giovanni Lauda

Client/manufacturer
Radice
1999

Three mysterious boxes; each one of them "compacting" both office environment and equipment. But it is not only computer equipment that is enclosed within these boxes: each becomes furniture within furniture, an inhabitable space, a rotating chair or a place to alternate between work and leisure time.

  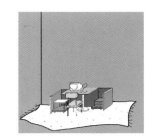 

We work, therefore, on few design projects, all chosen with extreme care. In fact we do not want to express style constants, nor originality at any cost. In our products we attempt to introduce innovative uses and to achieve not only formal but typological evolution, even by new combinations of archetypes and conventional languages. The innovation of our instruments for living adapts to technical, behavioural and consumption modifications, as well as being influenced by anthropological research.

In our research project of 1997 "Disappearing Acts" we tried to exemplify our ideas about dwelling. Here domestic activities are enclosed inside pullout components with standard dimensions: custom-made fully equipped boxes, furniture to live inside rather than around. By combining furniture and equipment, dematerialising and miniaturising them, we can concentrate resources and functions to obtain greater domestic mobility and more liberty in the undesigned space. For us the house is no longer divided into functional environments. New hierarchies and new relations can be established between domestic activities and furniture. An empty/dense space can combine new services and old rituals, conventional languages and new identities. In this way the home can be freed of expression and at the same time become more autobiographical.

Our studio is a small laboratory. By availing ourselves of young collaborators from all around the world, we are committed in the first place to projecting ourselves. We would like to define ourselves as "a small studio with big ideas". The many small Italian studios constitute a creative compartment for the service of industry. By means of this decentralisation, and analogous to the place of production, the studios represent the natural environment for the development of research for innovation.

28

dyson

Dyson Appliances Ltd
James Dyson

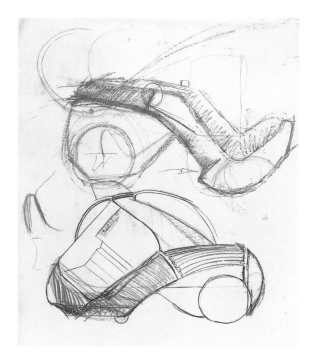

DC02 De Stijl

Cylinder Vacuum Cleaner
Dyson Appliances Ltd
1996

The Dyson De Stijl was created as a homage to the group and their radical use of colour to highlight the functional and geometric forms of an object.

Dyson started in 1992 as a group of six engineers who had trained as designers and decided to go into manufacture. We wanted to make vacuum cleaners using the new technology that we had developed, maintaining the integrity of our vision from this starting point right through to the production of a finished design which grew out of the product's function.

The studio has changed over the years in formal structure – from six we have now grown to 300 – and we've had to work hard to keep hold of this philosophy of design. We've kept the team atmosphere through the fluid use of groups working on different products. So, as we develop a new piece of technology a team will be working on that new technology, along with another team who work on engineering and designing the product. Each team is headed by a team leader, all of whom are graduates who've been with us for a few years. And I fit in as a kind of tutor, visiting each of the teams to see what's going on.

We've also added to that assembly of designers and engineers graphic designers, marketing people, patent lawyers and manufacturing people. So the entire team is "in-house" to ensure that the creative heart of the company really *is* at the heart of company, both philosophically and geographically. We don't want to be a part of the process of creating a new product: we want to be the whole process. This means that we can be creative in the fullest sense, creating the technology, designing the product, manufacturing the finished item, and then looking at service issues to see how we can refine our designs to make an even better model. And this is true as much for the individual as for the company. We don't have a distinction between the functions of product development – so that designers do scientists' work, and scientists end up doing what might normally be seen as a designer's work. Everyone has a say at every stage. For me this ability to become involved in every minutiae of a product is much more deeply satisfying than being partially involved in a variety of design projects.

DC04 Absolute™

Upright Vacuum Cleaner
Dyson Appliances Ltd
1999

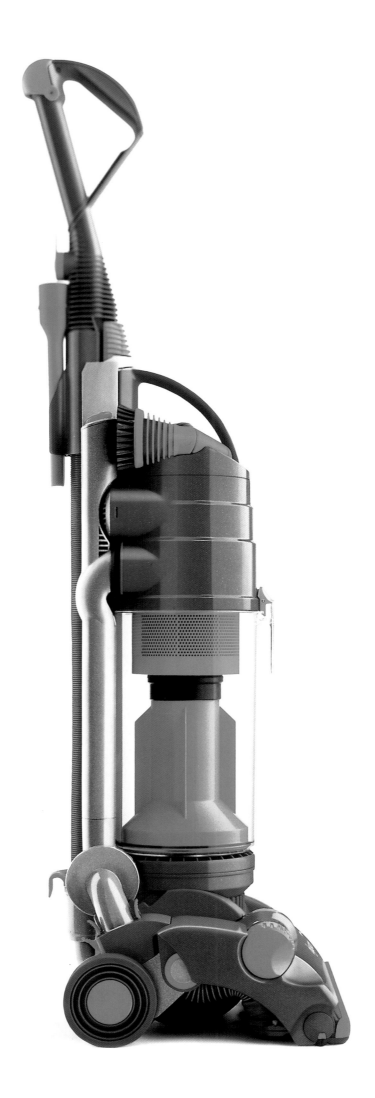

DC03™ Clear

Upright Vacuum Cleaner
Dyson Appliances Ltd
1998

The new R&D centre at our headquarters near Bath has an interesting set up, where engineers work right next to the laboratory, and the laboratory is right next to the machine shops, and so on in sequence. We even have glass windows, so it is easy to see what is going on between the areas, and people feel that they can just pop in. It's a very direct form of communication. We worked hard to avoid isolation, because as you get bigger this kind of cross-fertilisation gets harder and harder. Even the layout of tables and chairs has been thought out to promote a sense of inclusion. Each team works in an area perhaps ten metres by ten metres, with a huge circular table in the middle so that people can lay out drawings and prototypes and get together in groups to discuss things. Any discussion about a product is done in the middle, and everyone who is working around the edge feels that they can contribute to any meeting, even if it doesn't directly affect the bit that they are working on.

The touchstone of our design philosophy remains as generating ideas for technology that will make something perform better. Sometimes we've started out with the aim of developing new technology to do this thing better. In other cases we've realised how a bit of technology could be used if we could improve and adapt it. The technology itself can be almost anything; of the projects we're working on at the moment, many have common or related technologies to those we already develop, but at least two products use technology that is completely outside our current field.

I believe that if you want to stay around as a manufacturer you have to have this combination of strong technological research and manufacturing know-how. It is the way to generate real excitement and passion so that everyone involved can really see his or her contribution and strive to ensure the quality of the whole. And the result of this is that with luck you will make the revolutionary and surprising products that people really want and will go on wanting.

frogdesign
frogteam

Headset Study

Design
frogteam

Client
Plantronics
1998

"Kraftwerk meets anatomy –
a technology monument that
you want to wear."

Network Computer Study

Design
frogteam

Client
Oracle
1996

"An anti-PC information
appliance – in the optimistic form
of a 'plus' sign."

Each project that frogdesign undertakes has a frogteam attached to it, and each frogteam is unique. frogteams are not about any one single person or any one specific talent. They are of no predetermined size or make-up. They are flexible, constantly changing aggregates of frog's ethos that reflect both our internal growth and external (client) needs. Almost from the beginning, frog's founders realised that the complexity of design projects was growing, even as the time available to accomplish them was shrinking. Teamwork was not a luxury but a creative necessity, a way of accelerating individual efforts and a way of co-ordinating various urgent efforts across the spectrum of a project. During frog's history, frogteams have evolved from being a group of industrial designers with global backgrounds to being a truly interdisciplinary mix of design, engineering, branding and media talents. While other companies celebrate the egos of their star creators, frog has shown that inspiration is everywhere. If you want specific names for a project, frog would have to give you a complete employee list. At frog, everyone has a stake in a project's success – and that fact is the genesis of the frogteam approach.

In the 70s and early 80s, frogdesign was the first design company to truly advertise itself. It was the first to visually embody its brand. It was the first to grab the back cover of "form" and "iD", and shortly thereafter, other global design magazines as well. It was the first to get a "million dollar contract" (with Apple in 1983) in Silicon Valley business history, but it also was the first to re-invest into computer-aided machining tools. It was the first to see the global trend toward digital consumer electronics/personal computer convergence. And, in the 90s, it was the first of the major product-centric firms to catch web fever and ride the Internet wave. While frog was hatched in the land-locked netherworld of the German Black Forest, it was destined to surf the world!

From its Schwabish roots, frog expanded first (in the 80s) to Silicon Valley, and then it moved fairly rapidly (in the 90s) into the Silicon Prairie of Austin, Texas; Silicon Alley of New York; Media Gulch of San Francisco: and, most recently, along the Silicon River in Dusseldorf. Temporary offices have opened and closed in Tokyo, Singapore and Taiwan – all in keeping with frog's relentless reinvention of itself as a company.

frog is a lot like that old Frank Sinatra song about New York: If you can make it there, you can make it anywhere. At frog, you feel like you are at the centre of something big; and you want to be a part of it because if you leave too soon, you are afraid you will miss the best part. Because of its pace and pressure, frog is the hardest, coolest place to work that I know of. It gets great projects from the biggest and best clients but the stakes are always immense.

To its credit, frog has taken the time – and spent the money – to develop a company-wide "environmental corporate identity". As a result, it is a creative office that feels creative. The same eco-palette of materials is used in each location, and the offices are like one big pin-up; sketches and models are everywhere. Visualising ideas is at the core of everything we do, and because of that, frog always looks like a place that is in the process of becoming or transforming into something else.

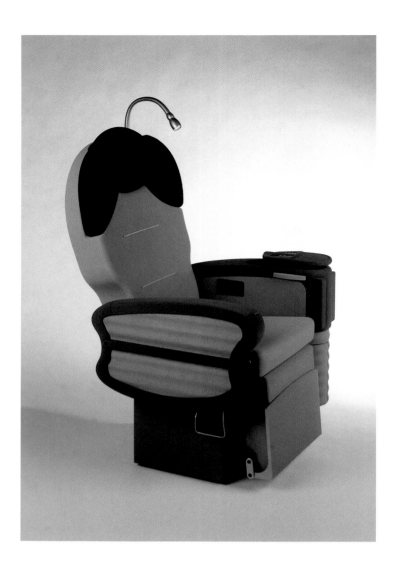

Lufthansa Airlines

Business-Class Seating,
Frankfurt International
Terminal Counters, Lounges
and Signage

Design

frogteam in cooperation with
Michael McDonough
Architect PC, Lori Wetzner
Design, Architektürburo
Belzner + Partners and
Timothy Stebbing

Client

Lufthansa
1996

"Re-capture the thrill –
reduce the stress."

HiFi and Consumer Electronics Line

Design

frogteam

Client

Karstadt / Dual
1995

"Familiar but strange – a new retro futuristic language that feels good."

We are trying to expand the definition of what a "product" can be (other than in the traditional sense of the term), which is why we are into strategic branding, new media work and even the design of environments. It is a way of expanding the problem or design brief – to enrich it and make it even more compelling at the same time as bringing even greater value and bigger success to our clients.

While we see almost every kind or flavour of project as benefiting from our product perspective and legacy of translating consumer needs into manufactured desirables, we also (at the core) are selective materialists and even sceptical consumers ourselves. Put it this way: frog founder Hartmut Esslinger freaks out when the media (or anyone else) refers to us as (merely) an "industrial design firm". While frog revels in making the newest and coolest things – we also know that those metrics are just the beginning point, not our ultimate design destination.

frog's most significant projects in the 90s brought together the right elements of creativity in the right sequence at the right time: for example, frog now brings together graphic design + corporate identity design + website design + industrial design + mechanical engineering + strategic branding + conceptual thinking reflected in specific industry knowledge and in application-specific points-of-view. This combination of services comprises our holistic, integrated way of designing – and is subject to further change as we (and our clients) grow.

In essence, "frog" began one night in 1969 after a jury review of a clock competition in Germany. The jurors were intent on venting their displeasure to the students, so they took the step of destroying some of the original models. Hartmut Esslinger, driving home later that evening, swore to himself that he would never behave toward new ideas with such fear and envy. He thought that starting his own firm would be his best revenge – and the most optimistic thing he could ever do.

frog was founded in opposition to the prevailing Modern sentiments of 60s Germany. Since then, frog has always stood for the best idea – the vision of what design could still yet become (as opposed to what it has already settled for being). From the beginning, frog was international in its outlook and saw the benefit of bringing Asian teamwork, European discipline, German precision, American optimism and Californian craziness together. It has also always been based on a team approach; frog has stood by this even with respect to crediting individual projects.

Finally, the "never leave well enough alone" mandate of Raymond Loewy has always had a place in frog's history. Whatever "it" is, it can always be done better. For a long time, frog has been a place for people who didn't quite fit in at other companies because they refused to give up their belief that they could change the world.

All of our best client relationships are partnerships of one kind or another. We would be nothing without our clients; we owe whatever success we have had to them. This realisation has propelled frog to do "whatever it takes" (while staying within legal and moral boundaries) to achieve project success. It is not so much a "win at all costs" mentality as it is a willingness to sacrifice ourselves for a period of time for the benefit of the team, project, client and/or company. It's an almost religious dedication to the job, an opportunity to do the absolute best possible job on something.

Typically, clients don't come to frog when they already know what they want or when they are doing a healthy business. They come when they are unsure, when they are stuck and dead in the water, when they are jinxed by someone else's screw-up, or when they are sick and looking for a kind of "strategic doctor" for the collective visual disorders of their firm. When they come to frog they expect a breakthrough on schedule and on budget, thank you very much. As more of frog's work has become time and media based, frog has focused

**Disney Quest
Theme Park Kiosk**

Design
frogteam

Client
Disney
1998

"Cool like a cartoon –
trusted like an ATM."

Javad Positioning System

Design
frogteam

Client
Javad
1998

"From UFO to SITO –
Super Identifiable Technology
Object."

**Sub-Notebook Computer/
PC Companion**

Design
frogteam

Client
Vadem
1998

"Trick detailing, thin and silver –
who needs grey 6lb bricks?"

on the "brand", the "experience" and the holistic potential of each client. In this way, frog's work has become ever more strategic, dealing with larger issues of corporate performance.

At frog we like change. Success. Successful change. How real people change products they own. New kinds of visual literacy. New kinds of beauty. "Beautility." Enabling people. Turning people on. Having "aesthetic mind-melds" with other like-minded types. Expressing speed. Achieving speed. Defining and re-defining quality. Showing everyday people – and allowing them to share in – the power of design. Integrating design and media in new ways. Envisioning not-yet-existing hardware and software partnerships. Customisation scenarios. Post-Market Product Alteration scenarios. Popularising new technologies. Exploring the cultural limits to success. Standing for something. Greenness in design. Designs that our children won't hate us for later on. Teaching part of the new generation. Remaining optimists. New models for the design practice. Giving away what is most precious. Further integrating the kinds of creative services that designers can provide. Telling stories through design. The overlap between products and services: provices and serducts. Working from "a spoon to a city".

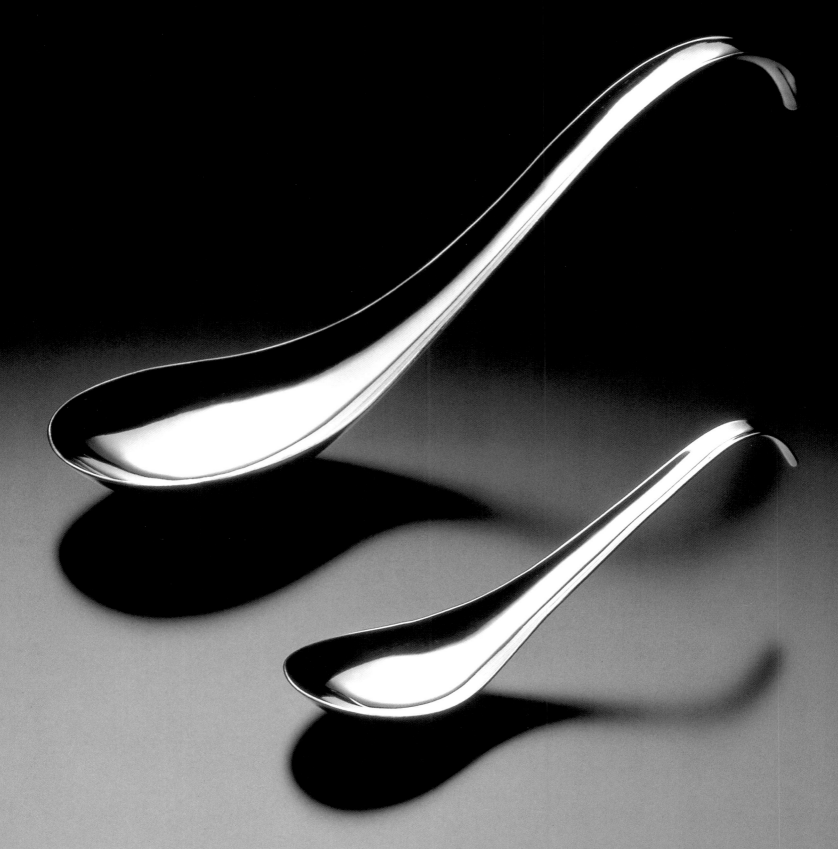

gk

GK Design Group
Kenji Ekuan

Design for Gift

Soy Sauce Dispenser

Design
Kenji Ekuan, Miwako Itoh

Client/manufacturer
Kikkoman Corporation
1961

The tool is a mirror that reflects people's way of thinking and feeling. To give a material thing is to give one's heart. A gift is a package of beautiful relationships between people.

Simplicity-Complexity

Tablespoon

Design
Kenji Ekuan, Kazutsune Tatsumi
1976

What is complexity-simplicity or simplicity-complexity? Simplification of complexity is made possible by developing and maturing the process of operation. It is a simple integration of complex fantasies.

GK Design consists of ten subsidiary design offices in locations such as Los Angeles, Amsterdam and Qingdao in China. There are 250 members – designers, specialists and administrators all working together. We cover a wide range of work from package and graphic design, product design, environmental design and data processing design – all under the umbrella of a global, freelance design office. As a result we benefit from many location specific opportunities including local information gathering for product export.

GK focus on three criteria – "Business, Promotion, and Research" – to propel its creative activities. "Business" is not only our bread and butter but it also gives us a real opportunity to put forward our thoughts to society; "Promotion" develops our profession's value in society; "Research" encourages us to develop our theoretical view of design – backing up Business and Promotion. We hold a convention of the design group once a year, as well as an internal presentation forum of projects, named "GK Gallery," in which our designers exchange their approaches and views three or four times a year.

To me, product design creates an opportunity for communication between clients and designers to users through formative expression. Design should contribute to man's spiritual development as well as advance technology. I believe that an ultimate goal of design is Truth, Goodness, and Beauty. People have been developing technology in an attempt to make it serve their well-being. However, it cannot necessarily do so as everybody recognises broken promises in our global environment. Nevertheless, more often than not people have failed to recognise technology's contribution in bringing a kind of democracy to our material world. From an historical point of view, the "comfort" of daily life in the material environment had been unfairly distributed. However, technology has liberated this comfort with dramatic speed on a global scale. I define this phenomenon as the "democratisation of the man-made world". My personal perspective of product design is that it is the struggle to make people comfortable in a built environment whilst ensuring that society remains sustainable.

Community Symbol
High Voltage Electricity Pylon

Design
Kenji Ekuan,
Matasaburo Maeda,

Design Group
Design Soken Hiroshima

Client/manufacturer
The Chugoku Electric Co Inc
1993

This symbol of power and the
new era also serves as a visual
symbol of the community.
A new interpretation of the
kind that used to be simply an
artificial steel structure
alienated from the
environment and human
communities.

Heart of Welcome

Bullet Train

Design
Kenji Ekuan, Yasutaka Suge

Manufacturer
Tokyu Train/Kawasaki Heavy
Industry

Client
East Japan Railway Company
1997

When preparing to welcome
an honoured guest, one
searches the depth's of one's
heart to choose objects that
reflect the respect felt for
this person. This is the heart
of welcome. Design that
expresses such depth of
feeling results in objects full
of grace, dignity and
character.

New Seed in Mobility

Bicycle

Design
Kenji Ekuan,
Yoshiro Yamakawa

Client/manufacturer
Maruishi Cycle Industries Ltd
1996

Through the ages, various
new species of vehicle have
been born and bred. They
have created new ways of life.
This is the result of enabling
vehicles to adapt to changing
environmental conditions –
which in turn makes new
demands on the environment.

I was born in 1929 into a family of Buddhist priests going back many generations. I was brought up in Hiroshima and was deeply influenced by the sight of it when it had been devastated by the atomic bomb. When I went back to the town it looked like no man's land: there was nothing but a land levelled to ashes. Capsized skeletal remains of the street trams and other charred things lying there against a backdrop of a red sunset seemed to me to be like dying creatures that were screaming out to be rescued. There and then I made up my mind to serve people and their environment, by reconstructing my country through design.

I graduated from the Tokyo National University of Fine Arts and Music, and the Art Center College of Design (USA). After coming back from the US in 1957, I organised a freelance industrial design office with several classmates and GK Design has developed from there.

If we view products as a species, we need them to have some way of working together to serve all the varied aspects of our daily lives. Good co-ordination might also encourage a comfortable and vital spiritual environment. A product with such characteristics may become very popular – but it has to be a reflection of the relationship between people and the built environment. A product has to reflect the attitude of the manufacturer and designer towards consumers and societies so it is essential that the client agrees this definition with us at the outset – we spend a great deal of time ensuring that this is the case.

Design needs a new definition and capacity to respond to human needs that are evolving in our rapidly changing social environment. This will only happen via more inter-disciplinary co-ordination with other professions. What I am most interested in is the co-existence of humanity and nature – in other words, the co-existence of nature and the high-tech environment.

Man-Machine-Soul-Energy

Motorcycle M11/Trial Model

Design
Kenji Ekuan, Atsushi Ishiyama

Client/manufacturer
Yamaha Motor Co Ltd
1991

This motorcycle is a machine
for pleasure. When man and
machine merge into a single
entity, the human soul comes
alive.

Immediately after World War II, in the midst of an overwhelming flood of American culture that came to Japan, "Tarzan" and "Blondie" comic books left the greatest impression on our generation. These comics unintentionally showed a dilemma of civilisation in which people had a profound longing to go back to Mother Nature and yet liked having the daily comforts brought by civilisation. This provocative dilemma still remains and awaits our response. I think that the true mission of technology and design should be the convergence of that dilemma for man's well-being as a whole.

I am also very interested in a "not so crazy idea" for the space age: in the future, a convention and an exhibition are held on the moon. The participants are impressed by the beauty of Mother Earth and are reminded of civilisation and culture, they thus realise the importance of acknowledging themselves as "creatures from the planet earth". The first time this happens, they come to know who they are by seeing the earth from outer space. One is oneself but one is not alone, so one is not oneself. It is a situation that reflects a sort of Zen-ist point of view. So amazement at and recognition of human scale and our environment may alert the world to the real goal of civilisation and design.

The images I have chosen are not a monotonous and incomprehensible survey of the product design process – but illustrate our concepts and design ethos. They are not sequential nor are they intended to be read as illustrations in a merchandise catalogue.

hollington

Hollington

Geoff Hollington

Proficia

Internet Telephone Handset

Design
Geoff Hollington,
Richard Arnott

Client
Camelot Inc (USA)
1997

This is the "mouse phone". It
sits on the desktop next to
your computer and works
with Internet telephone
software.

Trumpet Vase

Home Accessory

Design
Geoff Hollington,
Jacqui Wilkinson

Client
Design Ideas Inc
1996

This is a favourite, designed
for a Midwestern home
accessories company. The
combination of glass and
rubber is practical and looks
and feels quite special. The
tiny inscription says "Pardon
is the choicest flower of
victory".

At the Royal College of Art in the 70s I became good friends with Ben Kelly. We rather shunned the project work we were given. Instead, as "Ben and Geoff", we rebuilt the RCA's Junior Common Room, re-named it the Art Bar – which is still its name – staged RCA fashion shows and experimented with ideas about art and design. We just assumed you were supposed to do stuff like that.

That sense of being a bit to the side of the mainstream persists in the Hollington studio ethos. We try to avoid clients who want me-too products; we would rather our clients became providers of superior, more innovative products and services. I sometimes say to our clients that we are interested in history – what have we lost that was good? – and the future – which is when the things we are designing now will be introduced. But we are less interested in the present moment. We call ourselves the thoughtful design firm.

Our studio space in Shoreditch on the east side of Central London is a tall, vaulted, 1865 Gothic schoolroom where the children of workers in the local furniture workshops once studied. The neighbours now are designers, photographers and architects and we are surrounded by galleries, restaurants and bars. We have an open and collaborative studio atmosphere, helped by the fact that we sit around a huge central table (though it's so loaded with twenty-inch monitors that we can hardly see each other) and the space, which has enormous, church-like gothic windows, straw-coloured brick walls and two large trees. Apart from that it's rigorously contemporary and businesslike. Our team of men and women comprises mostly industrial and interaction designers by qualification, but we promote a spirit of generalism and connection making and can often bring our individual passions – which include music, writing, history and science – into the mainstream of our work.

At Hollington we thrive on variety, always looking for new product categories to conquer. It makes sense for our clients too, since lessons from one category can be applied in another, with no danger of conflicts of interest. Current projects include cameras, digital TV hardware, an office chair, bathroom fittings, an e-commerce website, a strategy for product user-interfaces, pens and 90 interactive exhibits for a science museum.

Industrial design has always been a multi-disciplined, inclusive activity, all the more so with the introduction of high-tech, computer-based design and engineering tools. "From Art to Part" is the catchy phrase used to describe the way designers can now use technology to drive a design all the way from the first pencil sketches

47

Hollington™ Chair
Office Seating

Design
Geoff Hollington
Client
Herman Miller Inc (USA)
1990

The Lounge Chair belongs to a group of "executive seating" for the new class of executives that emerged in the 1980s: younger, fitter and, likely as not, female. We wanted ergonomic excellence in a refined and elegant package with no overtly mechanical or high-tech details. This is not a "boy's toy" product.

48

Yoyo

Contract Seating

Design
Geoff Hollington,
Chris Dolan, Liz Ciokajlo

Client
Lloyd Loom of Spalding Ltd
1996

We suggested to the client
that the unique Lloyd Loom
material, which is woven from
a twisted paper yarn, would
be perfect for a collection of
contemporary seating. The
brown paper colour of the
natural material combines
beautifully with natural beech,
tan leather and silver
metallic-coated metal.

MSc Chair

Design
Geoff Hollington, Liz Ciokajlo

Client
SCP Ltd
1994

Sheridan Coakley at SCP
wanted a simple, low cost,
stacking chair. The all-steel
design is painted in one piece
after welded assembly.

Alu-1

Sunglasses (prototype research)

Design
Geoff Hollington,
David Townsend-Elliott
1998

We designed these sunglasses in cast aluminium and soft plastic. They have a unique, screwless hinge.

to the digital data used for tooling. We've embraced these changes, made the technology investment and enjoy the process, but we do emphasise the front end, innovative, thoughtful part of what we do. If we can help our clients by taking on board some of the downstream CAD modelling and development engineering workload we are happy to do so, but I truly believe that the place where we add most value, as consultants, is in the first third of the project, where the ideas are conceived and reined in; where the product concept is born.

We don't get easy projects. Our clients are fighting to survive and prosper in a competitive and hazardous environment. Their starting point is rarely "we need a new product and it should do this, this and this". More often there is a business goal, perhaps to reach new groups of consumers, or to commercialise a new technology. They will call us in to help understand the problem and devise product strategies. Sometimes our broad perspective, spanning many different product categories, markets and geographic regions, enables us to suggest product directions they were not aware of. Then comes the brief, which is usually a list of mutually contradictory aims, such as: we need high quality yet low cost; to reach the market in record time with a product so well developed that it will rarely disappoint, let alone harm a consumer; to inspire with forward-looking style without losing a sense of history, a place in time. Charles Eames, one of the twentieth century's greatest designers, when asked if constraints were a problem for a designer, memorably said that, "Design *depends* on constraints." Great design often comes from difficult beginnings.

It's an exciting time to be an industrial designer. Modern materials technologies offer fabulous opportunities: we are working on a camera which will have a tremendously rich look and feel, through a layering of materials, colours and finishes. There will be soft-feel, rubbery plastic, stainless steel, metallic-painted plastic and translucent plastic with pigments that change colour depending upon view-angle. The problem is knowing when to pull back and be cool! Our great allies in this area are Linda Barron and John Gould, a consulting team specialising in colour, material and finish design. They have helped us on products for Herman Miller, Parker, PaperMate, Cable & Wireless and Kodak. We can assume that the trend for intelligent materials will accelerate and that manufactured products will become more complex and more integrated in design and function, more

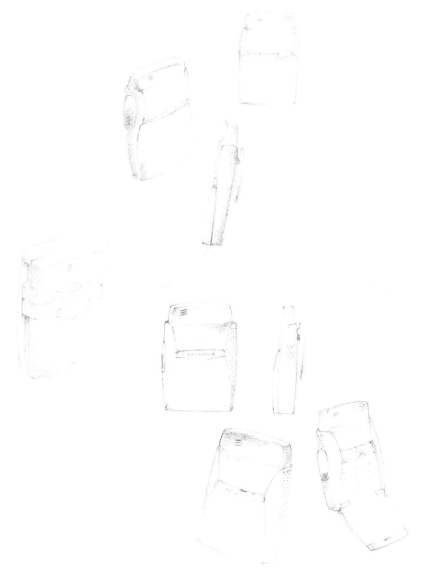

Design Language Study
Multi-media Document

Design
Tory Dunn, Geoff Hollington

Client
Ericsson Consumer Products
1998

A multi-media document for design language definition. We analysed Ericsson's mobile phone products to identify the common design elements that contribute to the familiar feel of the brand. The CD-based, interactive programme we created enables Ericsson designers to explore layers of brand language and speculate about how it could evolve and be applied to new products. This alternative to the old-style design manual is an organic, flexible and evolving design tool.

like plants and animals in fact. I agree with Eric Drexler (the controversial nanotechnology prophet) that at some time in the new century, rather than assembling products from discrete formed parts as we do today, we will learn how to grow them directly from their constituent atoms using chemical blueprints analogous to nature's DNA. Obviously this will transform the practice of design. Perhaps product designs will be allowed to evolve, virtually, in cyberspace, using programmes that simulate the Darwinian process. Designers – creative individuals – may still influence the process, but it is not clear exactly how.

Another compelling trend in product design is the convergence of hardware – made from atoms – and software – made from digits (Nicholas Negroponte of MIT's Media Lab coined this atoms-digits distinction). More and more kinds of products are born with an embedded computer chip (the "my toaster has more computing power than the first Space Shuttle" joke is almost true) and these on-board computers may need to communicate a lot with users. Design of the space where atoms and digits and people meet is called interaction design and providers of products and services often fail to embrace it effectively, which is why most people equate digital technology with bad ergonomics: mind-frazzling button-pressing and incomprehensible display menus. The really wonderful thing about interaction design is that it brings together so-called "hard" products, information technology, the Internet, home entertainment and telecommunications. We are helping to create the new Wellcome Wing at London's Science Museum where our job is to mastermind the development of around a 100 interactive exhibits, of which nearly half will be dedicated to the richness and potential of digital technology. This gallery will use digital techniques to talk about the digital subject. It's a huge challenge and a profound learning experience for our team.

A final word. We love to draw, in pencil, on paper. Despite all the computer kit and high-end whatnot, drawing is an important part of the Hollington studio culture. I have always found freehand drawing the quickest way to – literally – materialise an idea. You then look at the marks you've made and think again, and draw again, and thus a kind of feedback system is set up. I hope the time never comes when this process becomes irrelevant.

Mobile Player

Design
Thomas Overthun

Client
A

... Player for Audible is
... Internet Walkman for
... Download
... books or radio
... grab your player and
... press play. It sends a radio
... so you can throw it in
... car and listen through
... car radio, carry it with a
portable radio, or plug in
earphones.

ideo

IDEO Product Development
Bill Moggridge

SoftBook

Design
Joost Godee, Duane Bray

Client
Softbook Press
1998

The portable electronic book for SoftBook is designed to be a replacement for textbooks, business documents or reference books. It is an information appliance rather than a computer in that it connects automatically and directly to the web site when plugged into an ordinary phone line. It has an A4-sized display that turns on automatically when the leather cover is opened. A monthly subscription allows you to freely download books to read. A stylus is used to search and edit content, which is then stored in your own personal library at SoftBook Press.

Kodak Camera

Design
Mat Hunter, Nick Oakley

Client
Eastman Kodak
1997

The interaction architecture for digital cameras and other imaging products and services makes manipulating digital images easy and intuitive, and allows the camera user to concentrate on pictures and not process. The film strip idea on the little screen makes it easy to find the picture you want. The architecture is applied across the whole system, so that the user has a consistent experience, whether capturing, reviewing, or outputting images, networking with a personal computer, or setting preferences.

Products, Services and Spaces. IDEO is 350 people in ten locations around the world. We are dedicated to the innovative and user-centred design and development of products, services and spaces. Here is what Tom Peters, writing in "Forbes ASAP" says about us.

"IDEO is a zoo – oh, lovely metaphor for this age of the nanosecond! Experts of all flavors commingle in "offices" that look more like cacophonous kindergarten classrooms than home of one of the world's most successful design firms. Desks are littered with works-in-progress and the remains of midnight fast food binges. Models of futuristic lamps and movie special effects devices and high-tech blood chemistry analysers, in all stages of development, lie about here and there – and are the cause of nonstop kibitzing. The planet's most advanced software programs, running on the world's most advanced workstations, networked with heaven knows whom from heaven knows where, hum 24 hours a day."

Post-disciplinary. The challenge may be more than a product. It may be a system of products, or a melding of products with services or the space that can help people learn about the products. It may be an attitude; perhaps the tradition of a company is driven by technology, so the development teams seem to forget about the users; perhaps the focus is only on how to sell things, so no one thinks that much about the things themselves. Perhaps the difficulty is to understand the most significant challenge.

These challenges are confusing, and to respond to them we must thrive on confusion, being willing to experiment all the time with who does what, and how we do it. It's not enough to say, "Ask a designer" or "That's an engineering problem". Why should we plan and structure our efforts by discipline? Defining someone by discipline only tells you how people were trained, not what they can do now. What about everything they have learned since they left academia? What about that unique new combination of imagination and ability that only started to emerge when yesterday's challenge was met? The right combination may be Mat and Marion,

Kiss Communicator

Design
Duncan Kerr, Heather Martin
1998

This exploration allows an exchange of emotional information between two lovers, by creating a handheld device that sees the pattern in a blown kiss. You blow on the central slot and the electronics translate the impulse into a series of pulsating lights, which are then transmitted to your partner. Your partner far away sees a slow glow on an equivalent device, showing that a message has arrived. Unless it is touched, it will fade away and be gone, but if it is picked up and squeezed, it will play a repeat of the message that was transmitted, but in complementary colours. The ephemeral message plays back only once and, like a wave across a room, or a touch on the arm, is not stored or retrieved in any electronic form.

with some of Duncan's time, with solid analysis from Ed and wild flights of fancy from Blaise. Let's start with three quick brainstorm sessions and a deep dive. That should make heads spin, and lead us somewhere that we've never been before.

The context for this kind of approach to design is not defined by discipline, nor by multidisciplinary teams; rather it is by what people can *do*. IDEO is now made up of groups of people who come together because they are excited by and adept at a particular kind of work. They work in "post-disciplinary practices".

Information Appliances. The camera is a good example of an information appliance. Just a few years ago, a camera was a mechanical and optical instrument with a chemical film. Little by little the computer chips invaded. First it was automatic exposure, then auto-focus, and red-eye removal; now digital memory is replacing film. We still think of it as a camera, though, dedicated simply to the task of capturing images. Contrast that to a personal computer, a machine that is trying to do so many things that it stands no chance of doing any single one of them in a simple and easy-to-understand way, like an appliance.

Our post-disciplinary design teams are thriving on the challenges of creating appliances in places where chips can help to get things done. For Kodak we developed an Interaction Architecture, designed to help people play with digital photographs "in camera", rather than having to wait for the good and bad surprises to come back from film processing. The first version on the market was applied to the DC210 camera, a top seller even in Japan. This success was attributed to its ease of use.

An electronic book for SoftBook Press connects directly to your own net files through any phone line. You can browse around an on-line bookshop, and download the material that is relevant to a particular subject. The cross-references are easy to find, plus you can highlight and annotate. The text is not yet as enjoyable to look at as the printed page, but the speed of learning makes it worthwhile for work at least.

The Kiss Communicator is an experiment with messages between lovers. The elliptical shape fits into your hand. You blow into the central slot and the electronics translate the impulse into a series of pulsating lights that are transmitted to your partner. The ephemeral message plays back only once.

Digital Radio

Design
Tracy Currer, Nick Dormon

Client
BBC
1997

This exploration for the BBC examines the opportunities that can come from new digital radio transmission technology, and demonstrates them as scenarios of use, showing the potential to content providers and radio manufacturers. This scenario shows a radio that is shared by everyone in the family, so that program choices are made visible and new services with interactive audience participation are offered.

Tele TV

Satellite Antenna

Design
Martin Bone

Client
Tele TV
1997

This distinctive satellite antenna differentiated TeleTV from competitors by an appearance that is not just another satellite dish. The shape expresses a combination of high tech functionality with organic forms found in nature, inspired by the aerodynamic shape of a sea bird's beak, blended with the hydrodynamic face of a blue whale.

SyncMaster 400/500

Flat Screen Monitors

Design
Chris Loew

Client
Samsung
1997

IDEO provided industrial design for Samsung's SyncMaster 400 and 500 TFT LCD flat screen multimedia monitors. The elegant design emphasises the monitor's thinness and high quality, and features a unique conical-shaped base with built in speakers. The product has garnered significant worldwide recognition, including winning Korea's highest industrial design award.

Gripper
Toothbrushes

Design
Thomas Overthun,
Paul Bradley

Client
Oral B
1996

These toothbrushes for children feature a "Squish Grip" proportioned for smaller hands. Typical Oral-B elements, like the raised ridges on the front and back of the handle, have been reinterpreted in a playful, more childlike way. The design of the Gripper improves comfort and control of the brushing process with its unique shape and use of material.

Interactive Keyboard

Design
Takeshi Ishiguro,
Hector Moll-Carillo

Client
Yamaha
1997

The orange, yellow and blue buttons on this interactive keyboard for Yamaha are coded to the selection of tunes and rhythms, and presented in instrument groups that are indicated by icons, so that children can experiment with and enjoy sounds without needing any skill with the piano keys. This can lead naturally into learning to play the keyboard.

Nike Sunglasses

Design
David Tonge, Joe Tan,
David Peschel

Client
Nike
1997

IDEO developed a family of all-terrain eyewear with Nike, to provide sunglasses that help athletes to see where they are going across all types of country. Wrap-around lenses increase downward and peripheral fields of view and the "flying lens" design improves airflow and decreases fogging. The glasses employ a flexible frame to better fit a variety of head sizes, and a rubberised nosepiece provides better stability and comfort.

  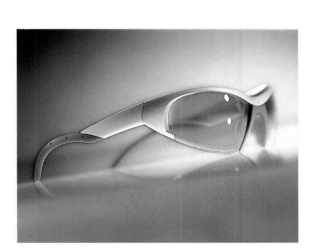

A Design Place. Designers still want to talk about the latest and most beautiful objects. Engineers still want to compare notes on ingenious mechanisms. This new world of post-disciplinary practices mixes everybody together in ways that stimulate and cross-fertilise, but sometimes makes you miss your peers. We want it both ways; both practices and peers, so that we can advance our specialist ideas as well as mixing it up. The Design Place is an antidote to the mix. It is a place where people come to sit and chat, to read magazines, and to see the latest work. A virtual extension of the physical place keeps IDEO designers around the world abreast of new ideas and projects.

Experience Prototyping. "Prototyping spoken here" is the motto printed on the glass door of our machine shop in Palo Alto. We have big investments in CAD CAM around the company, including over twenty CNC milling machines, four of them multi-turret. This is the equipment that you need for making prototypes that help you know what the experience of using a mechanism or physical product will be like. But what about a piece of software like a digital camera, or a system of connected experiences like a journey, or a service like booking flight reservations on the Internet, or learning about an educational programme? Now you need some new techniques and equipment for prototyping the experiences.

We are in the middle of putting together a plan for new facilities and skills for "experience prototyping". They include programming stamp chips in tweaked BASIC, enactment workshops, "Informances", and video scenarios. We want to use anything that will make future experiences a little more real, so that we can learn from trying out alternatives quickly and often.

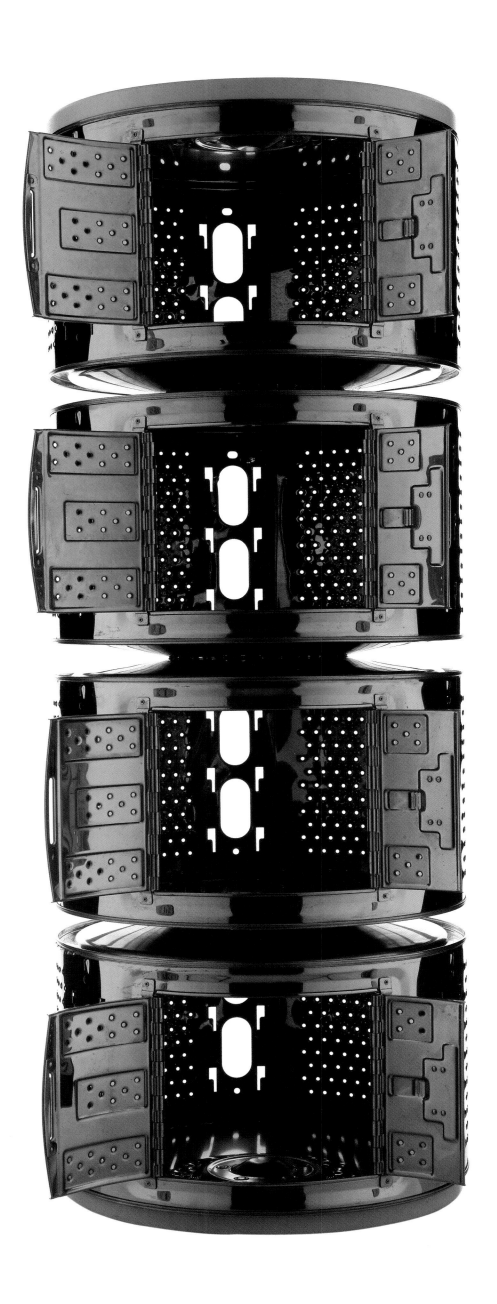

jam

JAM Design & Communications Ltd
Jamie Anley and Astrid Zala

Robostacker
Storage Cabinet

Design
JAM Design &
Communications Ltd

Manufacturer
Perigot

Photography
Sølve Sundsbo

Art Direction
Christian Küsters

Client
Whirlpool Europe srl
1995

JAM is a young company, set up only four years ago. We started simply, by redeveloping and reinterpreting existing products. Our first project was to take discarded cinematic film and realise its possibilities in another form: using the film as though it were a textile we made it into screens and lamps. Then we transformed traffic cones, ladders and washing machine drums into new products – tables, chairs, shelving, beds. Taking this approach we realised that we could look at any existing component or material and similarly design a new identity for it. Recognising also that the new artefacts we had produced retained some resonance with their first incarnation, we knew that we had chanced on something different. Not only were our designs fun in themselves, but unwittingly they reinforced awareness of the original materials when we exhibited them. We realised that our design work could be used as a communications tool in a very subtle, yet powerful way. The JAM philosophy came into being.

We decided to approach companies whose materials could be used to create products they had never considered before. Our first contract came from Zotefoams plc, whose industrial foam sheet material is used in the sports, automotive and packaging industry. We transformed its basic product into a wide range of domestic items and in the process alerted other designers to its possibilities, as well as boosting Zotefoams' brand image. This unexpected and unorthodox approach led to new markets for Zotefoams beyond its previous horizons.

We've worked hard to develop a new kind of organisation which communicates by design. We aim to be of benefit to our clients by changing the perceptions of the wider world through the unusual nature of our design work, which in turn gives their brand a revitalising boost. We collaborate with our clients rather than working to a set brief and in this way are free to be truly creative. We also collaborate openly with other designers (such as Fly, Yacht, Inflate etc) and encourage their participation in projects where their expertise is needed. This whole approach means that we have the ability to learn quickly as we discover new territory and we are constantly rewarded by input from clients and colleagues. A JAM collaboration can now result in anything from product design to interiors or sculpture, or sometimes just a play on words. Our aim is to produce something that expresses a corporate brand in a novel and thought-provoking way. The result is to push the boundaries of how we imagine things could be.

Over the years companies have relied predominantly on advertising to promote their products and brand image. JAM has now evolved a value-added method to enable their clients to express themselves in a way that taps into people's subliminal awareness. Not in a manipulative way, but rather by appealing to them at an "elemental" level. The designs that flow from our approach tend to have a positive resonance in a person's

Bulb Vase

Vase Made From a Light Bulb

Design
JAM Design &
Communications Ltd

Photography
Sølve Sundsbo

Art Direction
Christian Küsters

Client
Philips Lighting UK
1998

Moving Image

Stool Made From a TV Screen

Design
JAM Design &
Communications Ltd

Photography
Sølve Sundsbo

Art Direction
Christian Küsters

Manufacturer
Batch Product

Client
Sony UK
1995

Saturn
Two Part Suspended Light

Design
JAM Design &
Communications Ltd

Photography
Jason Tozer

Art Direction
Yacht

Manufacturer
Kewell Convertors

Client
Zotefoams plc
1999

consciousness because they work on both an unusual and yet reassuringly nostalgic level at the same time. They are also in the public domain for a great deal longer than a billboard advertisement or TV slot. Many items are in shows which tour the world for several years, some are domestic objects within people's homes and others are housed in permanent museum collections or illustrated in enduring works of reference. There is no need to just grab or buy the audience's attention because they become intrigued in a different way. Sometimes the public may even pay to see the idea, if it is in a gallery or exhibition. People are drawn to the concept because of its inherent fascination, because its eccentricity challenges their imagination and that is what gives it such force. Take the TV stool – yes, a stool made from a Sony TV tube – which has been purchased by the Guggenheim in New York as well as having toured the world. As a piece of furniture, it challenges its original function and as a sculpture, it transcends its recognised form. It has also resulted in both JAM, the artist, and Sony, the electronics manufacturer, being jointly credited for the value of the work. In the same way, a Philips light bulb glass has become a vase and SGB ladders have become a range of furniture.

We feel people are now in an exciting period of cultural change for which JAM's intuitive abilities are wel-suited. We have established our position in a new wave of thinking – as the pace and style of life changes, people will think in a new way and communicate in a new way. This is what excites us and it is where we fit in. We are pioneering a new attitude between our clients and their market audience – clients such as Sony and Whirlpool that need constantly to review the way they relate to existing and potential customers.

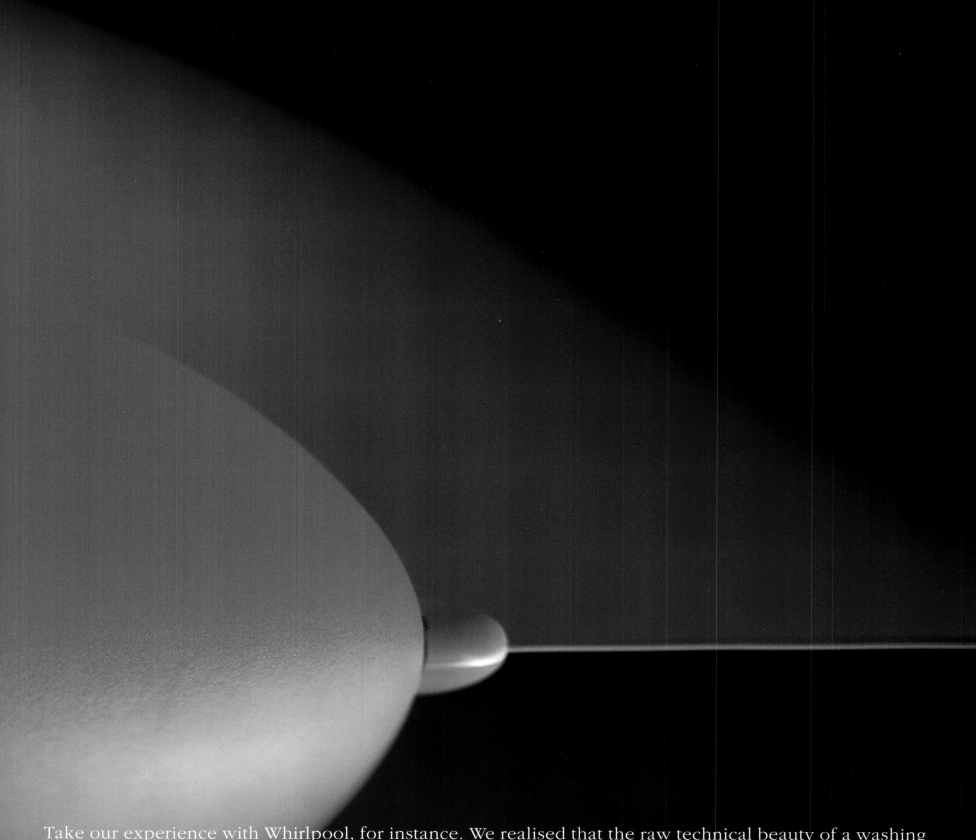

Take our experience with Whirlpool, for instance. We realised that the raw technical beauty of a washing machine remains unremarked, being unseen, but the superb quality of Whirlpool's stainless steel drums inspired us to focus on this component for our conceptual design. We saw that these items could have alternative functions as stools, tables and storage with only minor modifications. The engineering integrity of these components brings precision technology into the arena of domestic furniture. Now Whirlpool/JAM products are manufactured in France and Italy and distributed worldwide. They also continue to feature in many articles in both design and lifestyle magazines demonstrating the longevity of a striking idea beautifully expressed.

In fact, the media everywhere are excited by our work and seem to look forward to featuring our ideas. This media following means we can reach many more people and enables us to disseminate our ideas and elevate the brand image of our clients more effectively than traditionally used promotion methods. In the future, our aim is to expand our collaboration with companies as part of their overall marketing strategy, in conjunction with their advertising agencies and PR companies. Even some of the corporate dinosaurs are finding our style attractive. We are small, flexible and young, and adapt naturally to changing perceptions and innovations. Because of this, we are able to put our philosophy into practice to suit the personality of any client; we are not constrained by hierarchical corporate structures and have a "feel" for what's happening at ground level as a result of our open attitude with other creatives.

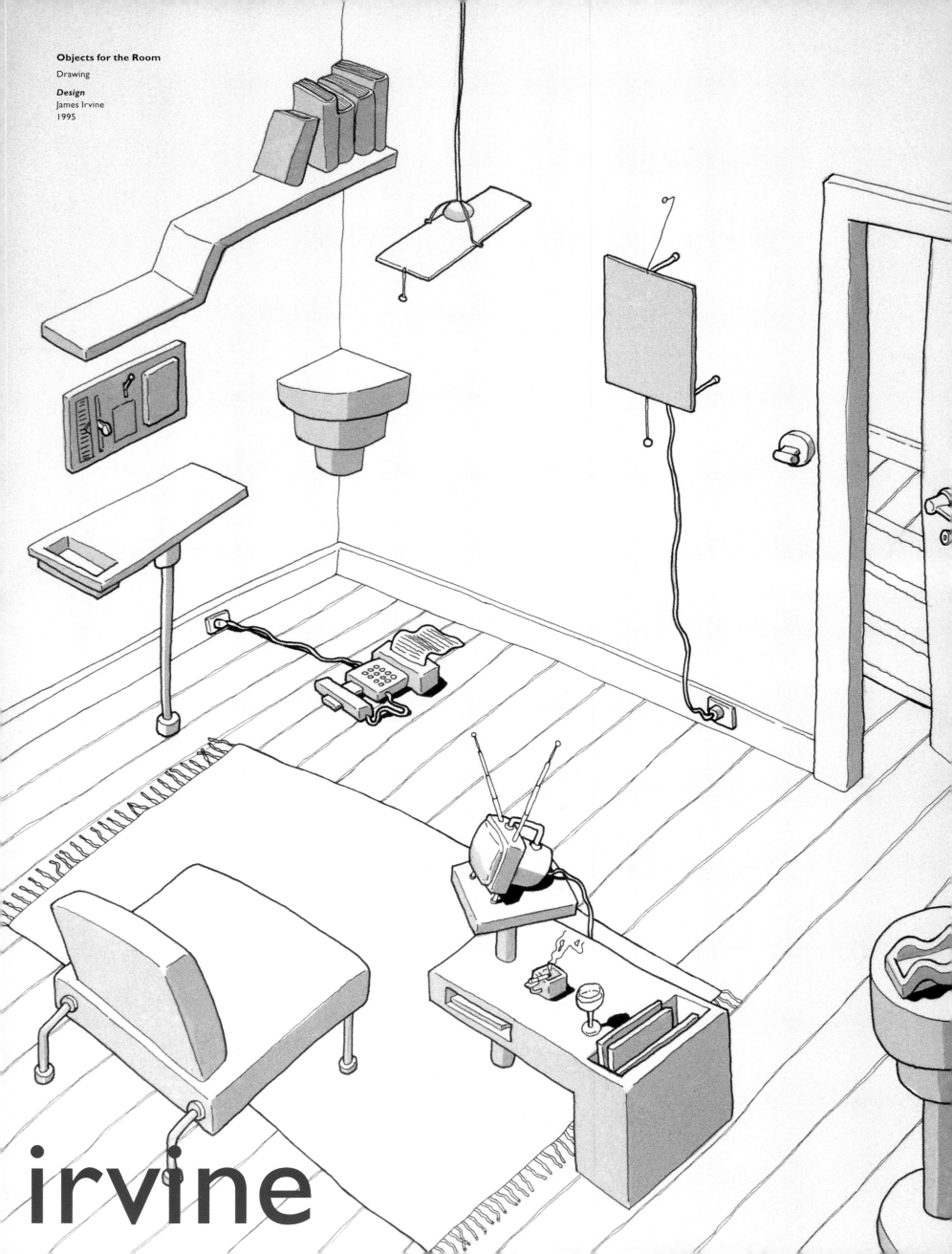

Objects for the Room
Drawing
Design
James Irvine
1995

irvine

James Irvine Design Studio
James Irvine

Tubo

Chair

Design
James Irvine

Client
BRF
1997

**Luigi
(The Waiter's Friend)**

Bottle Opener

Design
James Irvine

Client
ALFI 21
1999

Spider

Chair

Design
James Irvine

Client
Cappellini
1996

 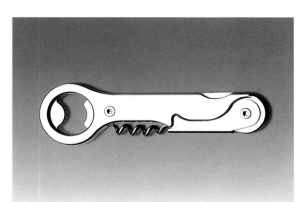 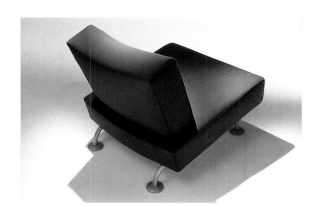

I have lived and worked in Milan for 14 years. I started out working for Olivetti and then in 1989 I went to work for Toshiba for a year in Tokyo. This was an extraordinary period of my life.

When I returned to Milan I decided to set up my own office because I had realised the importance of individuality and I realised I could be somebody in my own right. I carried on working for Olivetti but started doing my own private work on projects for companies such as Cappellini. Cappellini made some wonderful products and was one of the few companies that would give young people a break. Giulio Cappellini was, and still is, a great editor with the courage of his convictions.

One day Ettore Sottsass asked me to come and work with him as a partner. So I left Olivetti and for the following six years I ran the industrial design group Sottsass Associati in parallel with my own studio. Over the years we worked on some fantastic products – heavy industrial items such as ceramic toilets, bathtubs in pressed steel, office chairs and lighting. I gained a lot of experience in different industries and, as a result, have been running my own studio for a year.

Sometimes industry does not understand what a designer does or can do. Companies often see a designer more as a marketing tool rather than as part of culture or life. That's probably the main thing I learnt from Sottsass: how to get your thoughts across to industry rather than simply make a client money. At the moment I am designing a fleet of 100 buses for the city of Hannover. My clients are in fact the people of the city. It is an idyllic situation to be in because it is very rare today to be commissioned by the final user to create a product. The premise is not competition with other industries but rather to work within the context of what the people of Hannover need. Very unusual.

JI Sofa Bed

Design
James Irvine

Client
CBI
1995

 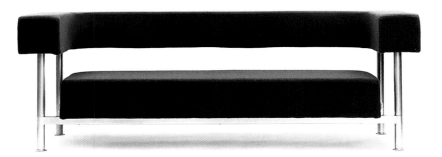

66

Living in Western society today, we are swamped with products and a glut of images, marketing techniques and advertising pushing products on to people. The "necessity" of things tends not to be an aesthetic discussion so most people talk about cost. This means companies like Ikea have enormous success, although it is basically making low quality products that do the job. At the other extreme people are prepared to spend incredible amounts of money to feel they are partaking in modern culture. For example, companies like Gucci and Prada etc. are really modern art forms. This reflects the desire of people to be "cultured"; to be players in the rotation of image and style. The middle ground is tending to fade.

When people see a product I would like them to understand its intrinsic value rather than it having a star quality or as something that is as cheap as possible. The very essence of an object for me does not come from shock or cheapness, it comes about from an extremely fine balance of different factors. You have to be modern, there is no doubt about that. However, modern things do not necessarily have to be weird. The defence of intrinsic quality today is important. Young student designers strive to shock because that is the only way they feel that they can put forward their identity. Industry often takes a similar standpoint.

Products today are part of everybody's life: they're in advertising, they are on videos, and they are on the street. On the day a new Audi comes out everybody knows almost immediately: mass communication occurs at a very high level. First you glimpse it on TV swishing down the Riviera and then you are driving down the motorway and suddenly you see it. It is rather like being at a public art opening. The difficulty is to design something that can survive in this context and have a "normal" quality – to find the right balance between being noticeable and devalued.

Lunar
Sofa Bed
Design
James Irvine
Client
B+B Italia
1998

I always found the discussion about minimalism – having been identified as a minimalist at a certain stage – rather frustrating. You could say that a circle is a minimal shape but that a circle is one of the strongest visual forms; it is dynamic yet simple. You can make something survive by reducing it to make it stronger. People are looking for stronger, simpler signs. This can be the case in any kind of product: furniture, a bus for a city centre or a bottle opener. The number of products available means that to design something that survives by its strength of simplicity gets more and more difficult, so you have to add other values. That is why things start to get a little silly. We design within the context of the competition.

We are not living in a decorative era, as far as I am concerned. Industry can create anything for us, the possibilities are so vast. One factor that has changed radically is that the hand-crafted object is behind us. The challenge for designers is to work with technology to find new aesthetics; this is constantly creating new possibilities. At the same time technology tends to reduce flexibility, so if you decide to produce something it makes economic sense to produce high volumes, and that creates another limitation. The furniture industry is one of the few areas where you can experiment without having these problems. That is why furniture in the Eighties and early Nineties was a reference point for what was happening in design. You could design without too many industrial limitations. Technical industries can do many things, but the level of investment usually forces companies to be extremely restrictive and careful about their research or to create something a little bit silly to get noticed.

Mind you, thank heaven for those silly and sane things. Think how boring life would be with only one or the other.

Stadtbus

City Bus for Hannover

Design
James Irvine

Client
Ustra/Mercedes Benz Evobus
1999

Jasper Morrison Design
Jasper Morrison

Lima
Outdoor Chair

Design
Jasper Morrison

Client
Cappellini
1996

Vitra Stacking Chair

Design
Jasper Morrison

Client
Vitra
1999

I enjoy working in London in a way that I don't think I would enjoy working as a designer in Milan. It's not easy to define why, but maybe it's because there is just very little of my kind of design going on here. I think British industry tends to gravitate towards bigger design groups; they see it as a service like advertising and consequently look for design agencies that are set up as "service providers". It's like the difference between supermarkets and delicatessens. Here we have only supermarkets, while on the continent there are mostly delicatessens. I feel like a delicatessen, offering something a little more special than a supermarket. In a country full of supermarkets, to run a delicatessen is more useful than it would be in Milan. I enjoy that difference.

Our studio is fairly laid back. I like to think over a new project before we start – there's an internal process that I need to go through before I'm ready to discuss what we should do. Having thought it over I usually sketch any ideas I've had. But there are so many different ways of arriving at a concept, there's no usual way: an idea might arrive and you know exactly what you're going to do with it, or it might take a lot of thinking, a lot of looking around and a lot of drawing before it's right. Mostly there's some drawing involved. Drawing for me is a way of putting ideas down on paper. The only problem is that when you start drawing you limit an idea and you've already marked the territory. So I only begin to draw when I'm pretty sure about my thoughts.

The process of drawing is somehow equivalent to working with another person. Once you've drawn it, you look at it, it comes back to you, you might make changes to an idea which could have seemed fairly developed in the thinking stage. Then it goes into second gear and at that stage you will have defined the product in your mind, you will have a feeling, you will know the atmosphere of the product.

Other than that the approach really depends on the project, If it's a job to design a gin bottle, then obviously one needs to find out about gin. Research is very much on-going. Everything is research, watching TV, flicking through a magazine, seeing an exhibition. This is input, which might be translated in some way into new ideas. It's about absorbing influences, good or bad. I'm not terribly diligent about attending cultural events, but when the mood takes me I'll go and see something.

Model-making. Again there are two types. There's the type which is necessary to do oneself, because it's a process of shaping that gives you the right form, like drawing, a kind of dialogue, but this time three-dimensional. With other projects it's a matter of working with a model-maker.

Try and be clear about what it is to be professional. I think if you leave college and get a job in a big design office that process gives you one sense of what it is to be professional. But if you work on your own from the

Tin Family

Stainless Steel Kitchen
Containers

Design
Jasper Morrison

Client
Alessi
1998

Op-la

Tray Table

Design
Jasper Morrison

Client
Alessi
1998

beginning, you develop your own sense of professionalism that is probably out of sync but is nevertheless a type of professionalism. If you walk into a big design office there will be a receptionist and you will probably have to sit down and wait to see somebody. In my case there isn't a receptionist and there isn't a secretary. On a shallow level we're not professional, but I think in other ways we are as professional as other design studios.

It's quite a mystery how we get clients. I have never actively sought them. There was one period around 1990 when I was out of work and I thought, What do I do now? That was the last time. Previous products bring in new clients, and new products bring in new clients. What you do now somehow defines what you will be doing later.

I want to maintain the variety of projects that we do here. There are projects that I would turn down, it depends how interesting they are. But I like to deal with very different projects at the same time. For example last year we were finishing the design of a tram, designing porcelain tableware, and working on a chair for a Le Corbusier monastery. I think this variety is very healthy. I'm also aiming to design things with a higher level of production, with newer technologies, technologies that allow bigger production. A project that would have been a wooden chair five years ago is now a plastic chair.

I think one of the mistakes that design has made in the past and is getting over now, is to try to be special, to design for design's sake. I think we should be designing normal products and there shouldn't be a boundary between design and normality.

There are some everyday objects which are much more successful than the "designed" objects which one might have given or bought. So, for example, you might be in the kitchen pouring a glass of water and suddenly realise that the glass you've selected, without really thinking about it, is a very special object. It is the right glass; it is the one you instinctively reach for when you want a drink. Or it could be a particular saucepan, or you sit in a particular chair. These are objects that might not be that noticeable but, which over time have proved themselves to be effective in their role.

If you design a doorhandle, it's infinitely more satisfying to see it on the door of a cheap bar, in a small village in the middle of Germany, than it is to see it in a four-star hotel, where you know an architect has selected it because it matches the wall lights!

Hi-Fi System

Design
Jasper Morrison, John Tree
(Sony Design Centre Europe)
Client
Sony Design Centre Europe
1998

Garbo
Garbage Can
High impact polypropylene

Design
Karim Rashid

Client
Umbra
1996

The objective was to provide the mass market with a highly unique, yet highly utilitarian wastecan, accessible at a very low cost. The product can be used in the home and office, is very lightweight and distinctive. The low cost was achieved by using polymers which are easier to mold and suitable for organic curvilinear shapes. The tooling costs were reduced because of the form's simple symmetry (curved cylindrical shape) yet the form still appears asymmetrical in appearance due to the way the top edge has been cut. The double walled base with a rounded interior, provides easy cleaning (no right angles for coffee etc to get into) and a heavier base for better structural balance.

Karim Rashid Inc
Karim Rashid

 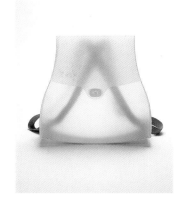 

Torso Bag

Flat polypropylene sheet with
injection polyolefin handle.

Backpack

Flat polypropylene with
silver nylon strap.

Hip Bag

Flat polypropylene sheet with
polyurethane handle insert.

Design
Karim Rashid
Client
Issey Miyake
1998

I think about the future too much. I saw a CNN report about perfectionists. Apparently they never live in the present. I never knew that. My mind is perpetually on the future and the problem with that is that every time I'm working on a project, I'm more interested in the one that might come along next. And the strange thing about that is that I put all my energies into the next project and, all of a sudden, three months later, I'm actually doing it.

The world of product design can be very dull. Really banal, because you're put under such phenomenal restrictions and limitations. The product design high-tech world is very conservative; loaded with bureaucrats and marketers. Concepts may start off exceptionally interesting but somehow they get more conventional. But things are changing and shifting now. New attitudes, new sensibilities and new energies are entering our product landscape. It's almost an awakening. There is realisation that a product can be uplifting, much more pleasurable, that it can bring more to life. I call these new objects "de-stressers". Rather than obstacles objects should be raptures of experience. Strangely enough, high-tech products have a 13-month maximum lifespan. So if you think about that short lifespan, then you think about the housing, the form of the object itself, its semantics and its behaviour could be anything, and ideally almost nothing. Objects could dematerialise. So why are they somehow relegated to becoming conventional 'grey' boxes?

Now things are changing because of the millennium. And millennium is a beautiful word because it's an excuse to start looking ahead. So, everybody's hanging onto this idea of the future, which is kind of what we went through in the 60s, when we were doing real aerospace experiments, and we thought we were going to land on the moon. The same kind of optimism as then exists now; the difference is that now we are in the digital age, which is really shaping our lives, our aesthetics and our sense of being.

R30 Chair
Askew Table
Ovoid Chair
Syntax Stacking Chair

Decola Vita Furniture
Collection

Design
Karim Rashid

Client
Idée Co
1998 – 1999

The material used in this new line of furniture posed many design limitations. Only six radii were allowed, and only two inner bending radii of 155mm and 30mm, as well as other restrictions in lengths and thickness. The development of this line used these to its advantage and created pieces that creatively use the material. Decola Vita compact forming laminates are duromeric high-pressure laminates with a special core-construction and a surface quality. Paper sheets impregnated with phenolic and melamine resins are the raw material for the production, pressed under high pressure and high temperature. Showing extremely high stability and being crash and impact proof, this laminate provides best facilities for any kind of heavy duty interior application, but also is physiologically unobjectionable, electronically non-conducting, does not corrode and practically does not emit Formaldehyde. Humidity resistant and the hygienic high-0 density surface complete the outstanding characteristics of this modern material and make the attractive surface easy to clean.

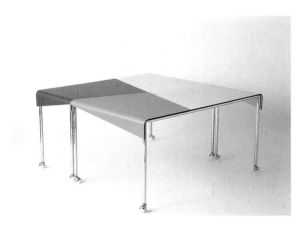

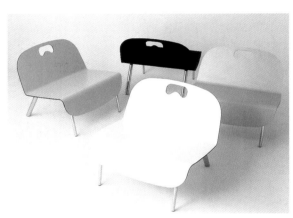

It's beautiful that people are talking about the future. Because, the 90s are so regressive. It's almost as if we're pretending that we don't know what the past was. It is easy to see that everybody's appropriating, varying and mixing history. So I think that the future – in terms of looking at globalisation and culture – looks optimistic because we now want to try new things. We want to experiment more. We want to change our daily lives.

In my work, I have three criteria. First, I need to do something original, or at least have some nuance of originality. I have to contribute something or there is no point. You get to the point where industrial design is just a service; it's not a creative process. I love industry and business but I was brought up by a family of artists with the notion that what is most important is ideas. It's about developing interesting content. It's about changing the landscape, somehow. I believe that design is extremely important to our daily lives where we impact on physical, physiological and social life and set up conditions of human experience.

Second, I believe my work is the study of alternatives and possibilities of commodities that affect society. I am the 'artist of real issues', of everyday life who mediates between industry and the user; between self-expression and desire and production technologies. Our lives are elevated when we experience beauty, comfort, luxury, performance and utility seamlessly.

Design is not as personal as art is, in the sense that you can have a message, and you can just put the message out there and disseminate it. But design is really a balance of the empirical and the visceral, the creative expression and commercial industry. Then the industry has to want to agree with your message, to disseminate

it. So it's much more involved and much more complex. At the same time every project that I do must be interesting, inspiring, and beautiful. I don't do anything I don't believe in. I don't put anything on the market that I don't believe makes a contribution. Because I think we have a plethora of products and we don't really need any more stuff, period. And I don't work with anybody I don't want to work with. I'm just trying to enjoy the experience of doing interesting things, and not fall into what I call the old school of industrial design that is a kind of styling service school – that to me is a really banal world.

There is a discussion about post-industrial design that suggests it is no longer about the individual, that the future of design development will be about teams. This is true because products are becoming smart. And if they're becoming smart, you need all kinds of players involved in the design process. If they become so smart, fuzzy, and intelligent, like the hyperobject you implant in your own eye, what is the industrial designer's role going to be then? You need a whole collaborative of other people: biochemists, engineers, behaviourists, and then the designer's role is based on experience, cultural shaping and human conditions. Yet, as a general rule it is one mind that inspires, that creates that original thought, that phenomenon.

I was once part of a team, and the projects we did were very team orientated, and I can't really work that way, because I'm an artist. An artist in a commercial field. Maybe I am too emotional. Real industrial design, in the wider sense is not about being emotive, it's not about being super-expressive, it's about doing your job, not cultural shaping. But I am determined to shape our daily lives.

Kismet

Salt and Pepper Collection

Design
Karim Rashid

Client
Nambé
1995

The Nambé Studio Collection
consists of 80 objects that
emphasise the need for
beauty and material, through
the soft, solid, ergonomic,
sensual, desirable forms –
that blur the familiar and
unfamiliar. The objects are
made of an aerospace mixed
metal alloy. The challenges
involved were to develop
beautiful objects that would
combine hand-craftsmanship
with sophisticated computer
technology, be efficient to
produce and cost sensitive,
yet of the highest quality. The
designs are the marriage of
'liquid metal' semantics and
solid heavy sustainable
material beauty. Some of the
objects are intentionally
ambiguous and organic to
afford personalised use.
The future of the designer
is to exploit production
technology. I am interested in
new materials, and stretching
the potentials of production
methods to create new
diverse objects. The creative
act is in this mastering of the
marriage of poetic ideas and
digital technology. Beauty and
simplicity will shape our
future objects in an
immaterial society.

Linea Collection

Crystal Vases

Design
Karim Rashid

Client
Nambé
1998

These pieces use an un-traditional undulating cut, which varies with each piece. The cut is perpetually changing, and a piece having several cuts thus creates the illusion of a forever-changing pattern of line. The pieces are unusually heavy due to the use of thick ice (ice refers to the amount of solid glass used on the bottom of the piece for stability) which is an important issue in differentiating qualities of crystal manufacturing. This reflects the high quality that Nambé is known for in their metal collection.

My third criterion is to align myself only with people and companies I respect. I am interested in building seamless relationships with industries. And that's what makes innovative projects happen. In the United States design tends to be a business form, not an art form. It is dipolar in Europe, but changing fortunately. As a designer I have learned in the most rigorous context. Sometimes I feel like a pioneer, yet America's entrepreneurism is phenomenal.

I believe that products must deal with our emotional ground and increase our popular imagination. Diversity, variance, multiplicity, and change are part of the whole of my constructs. I have a great love of inspiring neoteric things. I believe that the new objects that shape our lives are transconceptual, multi-cultural hybrids, objects that can exist anywhere in different contexts. They are natural and synthetic, inspired through telecommunications, information, entertainment, and pleasure. Our object culture can captivate the energy and phenomena of this contemporary universal culture of the digital age. The birth of new industrial processes, new materials and global markets are my great interests in design. They all lend hope to reshaping our lives. I feel new culture demands new forms, material and style.

lovegrove

Lovegrove Studio
Ross Lovegrove

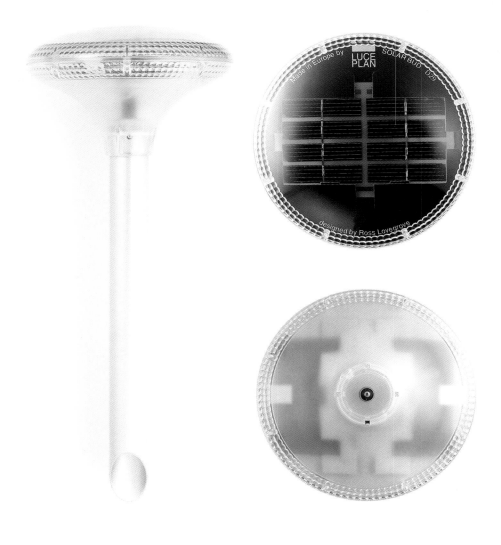

Solar Bud
Solar-Powered Outdoor Light

Design
Ross Lovegrove

Client
Luceplan Spa Italy
1999

Mass Individualism is the ultimate goal of the designer and the manufacturer concerned with qualitative consumer culture. Each and every product produced in quantity is to a large extent a carefully considered exercise in taste arbitration. Products are often conceived by individual designers, commissioned by manufacturers who value their cultural insight and recognise the value of emotional, functional and aesthetic transfer into the products we surround ourselves with everyday.

Consumer culture is a fact of life within which many view points and attitudes co-exist.

A modern designer must be sensitive to attitudes to materials, resource use, ecology, usefulness, beauty, craft and technology, if he or she is to respond to the task with intelligent solutions.

When well thought through, there is a beauty in mass-produced objects where the benefits are automatically transferred to many, creating a sense of positive global consciousness.

However, when products are manufactured for pure commercial gain without the creative virtue of respect for material resource, the effect not only lowers the physical perceived value of our habitat but also destroys consumer confidence in the creative process.

As we enter fully a new plastic age our sensitivity towards other materials and their potential to co-exist through industrialised or craft means will create a new texture for our environment.

It will also change our attitude toward the definition of the natural and the artificial world as boundaries are blurred by the intervention of science, genetic engineering and new materials technology.

Collectively, all we know is becoming subject to high-volume manufacture as a means of fulfilling the demands of an ever-expanding global population. Food production, packaging and the chain of events that satisfy our mass individualistic consumer needs also relate to the logic of manufacturing and the supply of sustainable, useful goods.

With this in mind a co-existence of collective aims and principles must be encouraged, accepting that mass production with a view to mass individualism is a logical path and one that should be celebrated as a natural consequence of man's inevitable adaptation of his environment.

Pod Lens

Design
Ross Lovegrove

Client
Luceplan Spa Italy
1999

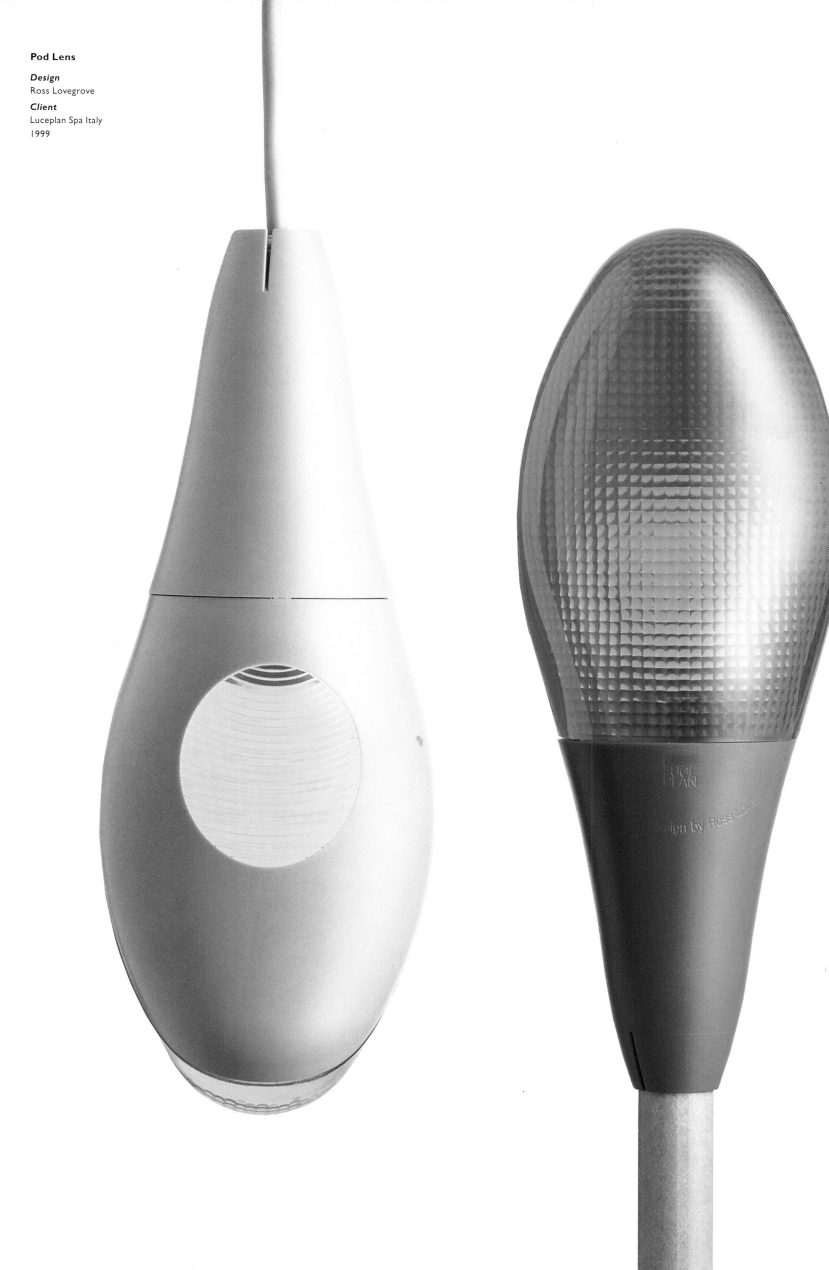

Ammonite
Communicator Study

Design
Ross Lovegrove

Client
Apple Computer Inc
1995

Photograph John Ross

Apollo (Q.W.E.R.T.Y.)

Rattan Chaise Longue

Design
Ross Lovegrove

Client
Driade Spa Italy
1998

Spin (G.E.O)

Design
Ross Lovegrove

Client
Driade Spa Italy
1998

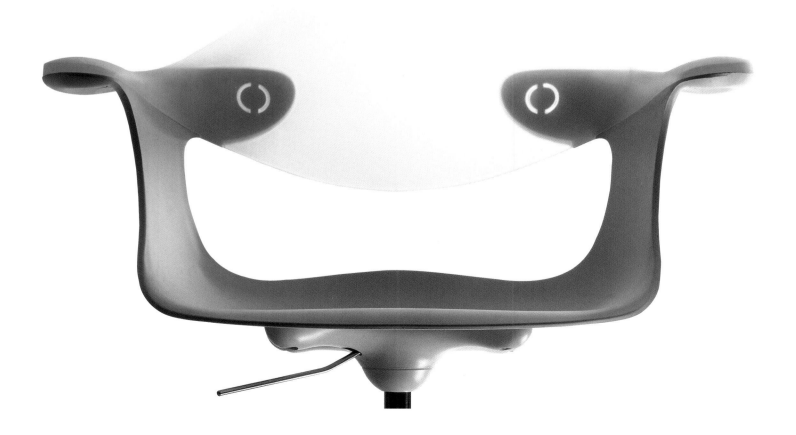

Kettle

Design
Ross Lovegrove

Client
Hackman Tools™ Finland
1999

lunar

Lunar Design
Jeff Smith and Gerard Furbershaw

Absolut Sillas Para Sus Bebidas

Bar Stools

Design
Jeff Salazar, Jeff Hoefer
Client
Lunar Design
1995

These two stools were designed for a competition sponsored by Absolut Vodka – and won the Grand Prize.

Lush Lily

Cocktail Trays

Design
Yves Behar, Jeff Hoefer, Darren Blum, David Malina
Client
Lunar Design
1995

Here in Silicon Valley, everyone is fixated on the future; every product must be smarter, faster, smaller, sooner. Although our jobs require us to address demanding technical constraints and market pressures, we are passionate about integrating art and culture into our products. The diversity of our staff, which represents nationalities from all over Europe, Asia, and North America, gives us a broad perspective and enables us to design for a global audience. At Lunar, we draw from many viewpoints, sources of inspiration, and histories to infuse products with human emotion and meaning as well as functionality.

Like most San Francisco Bay Area businesses, the work environment at Lunar is informal, egalitarian, and entrepreneurial. People dress casually and keep flexible hours. Neither of us would ever ask someone to do something that we wouldn't do ourselves, and we have an "open-door" management style that makes us accessible. Our employee attrition rate is low, the work quality is high, and the business is profitable, so we're on the right track. Our central mission is to ensure our clients' success by developing products that communicate the corporate brand message, engage and connect emotionally with the user, express and support functionality, and embody excellent craftsmanship. To achieve that mission, we subscribe to three basic assertions about the product design process.

First, design opportunities vary with the product life cycle. When new products create new markets, design can be edgy and unique or simply utilitarian. As a market grows, design must be innovative enough to help differentiate competitors and build brand awareness. And as the market matures and products proliferate, the design challenge becomes tailoring and targeting products to new segments. Understanding this naturally occurring cycle helps us to optimise the role that design can play at any given time.

Second, the key to successful design is to create an effective strategic conversation among the market, producer, and design team. Strategic conversation is the art of discovering, defining, understanding, and

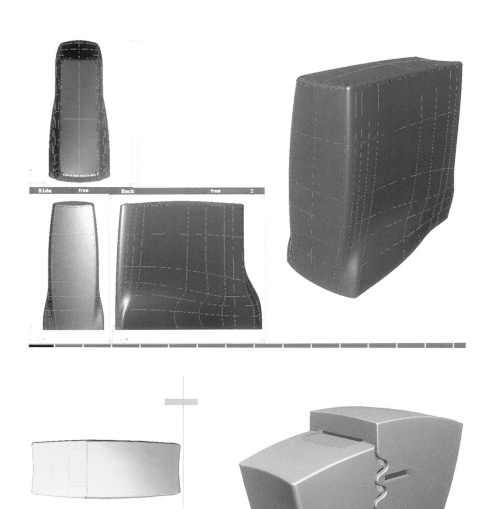

02 Workstation

Design
Jeff Smith, Ken Wood,
Yves Behar, Darren Blum,
Alex Von Wolfe, Jeff Hoefer,
Todd Lewis

Client/manufacturer
Silicon Graphics
1996

Silicon Graphics, a company
known for its leading CAD
technology, employed Lunar
to design its high
performance/low cost Unix
workstation. The design team
wanted to create a striking
and engaging appearance that
would be intriguing for the
majority of SGI's technology-
literate customers. Working
with CAD specialists from
Alchemy Labs, Lunar used
Alias to create photorealistic
renderings of the design
concepts. The final design
pushed CAD tools to their
limit but SGI succeeded in
developing a workstation
appearance that is a direct
manifestation of what its own
computer technology can
create.

90 articulating all the criteria necessary to bring the vision of a successful product into focus, and to do it in a way that's useful to the design process. We work with researchers to create an in-depth profile of the customer and to immerse ourselves in the marketplace. Ultimately, we develop a detailed visual map that correlates all of the design and research information and gives everyone a blueprint for moving forward.

Third, process alone will never make product design compelling; good design will always require talented artists. It's their job, after all, to summarise, synthesise, and distil all the raw material into a design that resonates with the market and outperforms its competitors.

New products don't reflect the future; they *are* the future. Product designers have always been charged with envisioning the future and making it real – with getting it out of people's heads and into their guts, with making it a visceral experience, and with sharing the experience so people can act on it.

When you think about it, product design is a metaphor for how you live your life. You combine the realities of the physical world, the influences of your culture, and your own inner voice to come up with something that works. That's how we've approached building Lunar, too.

Our design philosophy is to integrate the individual expression of art, the cultural tradition of craft, and the logical practicality of science. Reconciling those three elements is an exciting challenge. We always try to work in that grey area between the analytical and the intuitive. A successful example is the ergonomic CrossAction toothbrush we created for Oral-B.

The client's goal for the product-development programme was to deliver a manual toothbrush that could be clinically proven to remove more dental plaque than any other. Lunar's role was to enhance the ergonomics of the handle. This project was particularly gratifying. Through appropriate consumer research, teamwork, and the design team's intuition, Lunar helped Oral-B create a toothbrush that is highly ergonomic, aesthetically

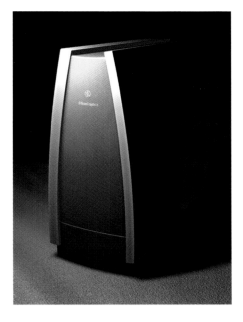

appealing, and projected to be a market success because it is so effective – something that consumers are willing to pay the highest price to use.

We work with a variety of clients, from large corporations to start-ups. We have satisfying, long-term relationships with companies that we consult with continuously, but we balance those with a handful of small clients whose products we find to be especially interesting or worth investment. Our goal is to move Lunar towards a structure that allows us to dedicate about half our time to traditional consulting services for market-rate fees, about one-third to equity-based opportunities, and the remainder to pro bono projects. We're also committed to becoming equally skilled in both design and engineering at all three phases of the product life cycle, from inception to growth to maturity.

As Lunar grows, one of our greatest challenges is to offer the benefits of a big design firm without losing our small-company style. We want to be responsive, offer a full range of services, and provide depth of expertise in specific areas. At the same time, we want the firm's principals to stay involved in projects and to retain a personal, community feeling in working with clients.

One way we've found to "work big" is to partner with market research and dedicated engineering companies such as Cheskin Research, Metaphase, Product Genesis, and Function Engineering. Together, we can take on complete product development programmes and add value at every step. We've also found it worthwhile to invest in venture companies, such as Modus Group, that offer associated services. We're always open to these kinds of investment opportunities. Lunar co-founded Satellite Models, for example. With these kinds of alliances, we can expand our capabilities and creative opportunities without becoming organisationally unwieldy. For us, it's less important to say, "Lunar did it" than to help our clients make the right strategic decisions and get the right business results.

Oral-B Cross Action Toothbrush

Design
Jeff Hoefer, Jeffrey Salazar,
Max Yoshimoto

Client/manufacturer
Oral-B Laboratories and
Braun AG
1999

The combination of the
design of the bristles, handle
materials (solid and
elastomeric resin) and the
fullness of the grip make it
obvious to consumers that
this brush is a high-end, high
performance product.

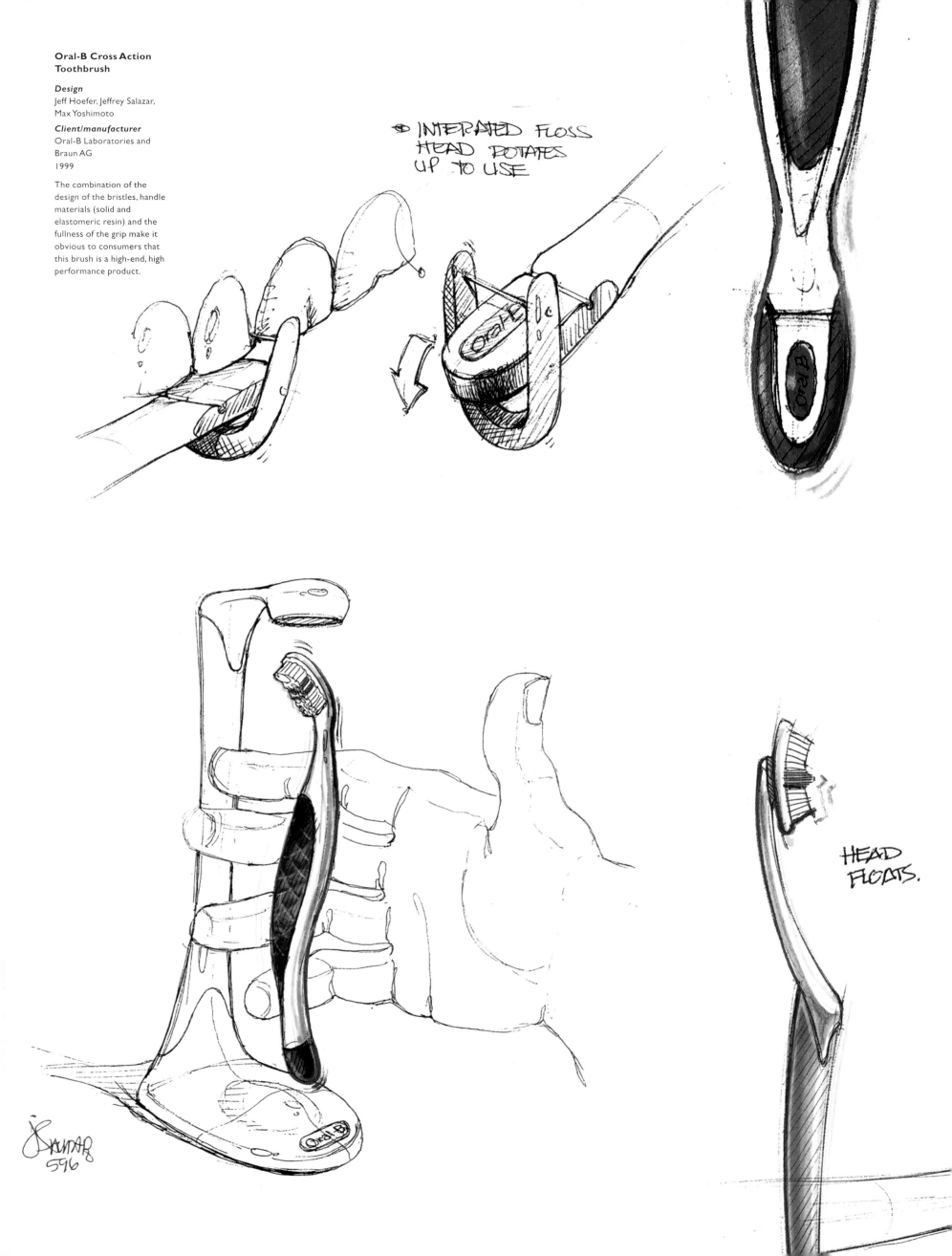

① INTERGRATED FLOSS
HEAD ROTATES
UP TO USE

HEAD
FLOATS.

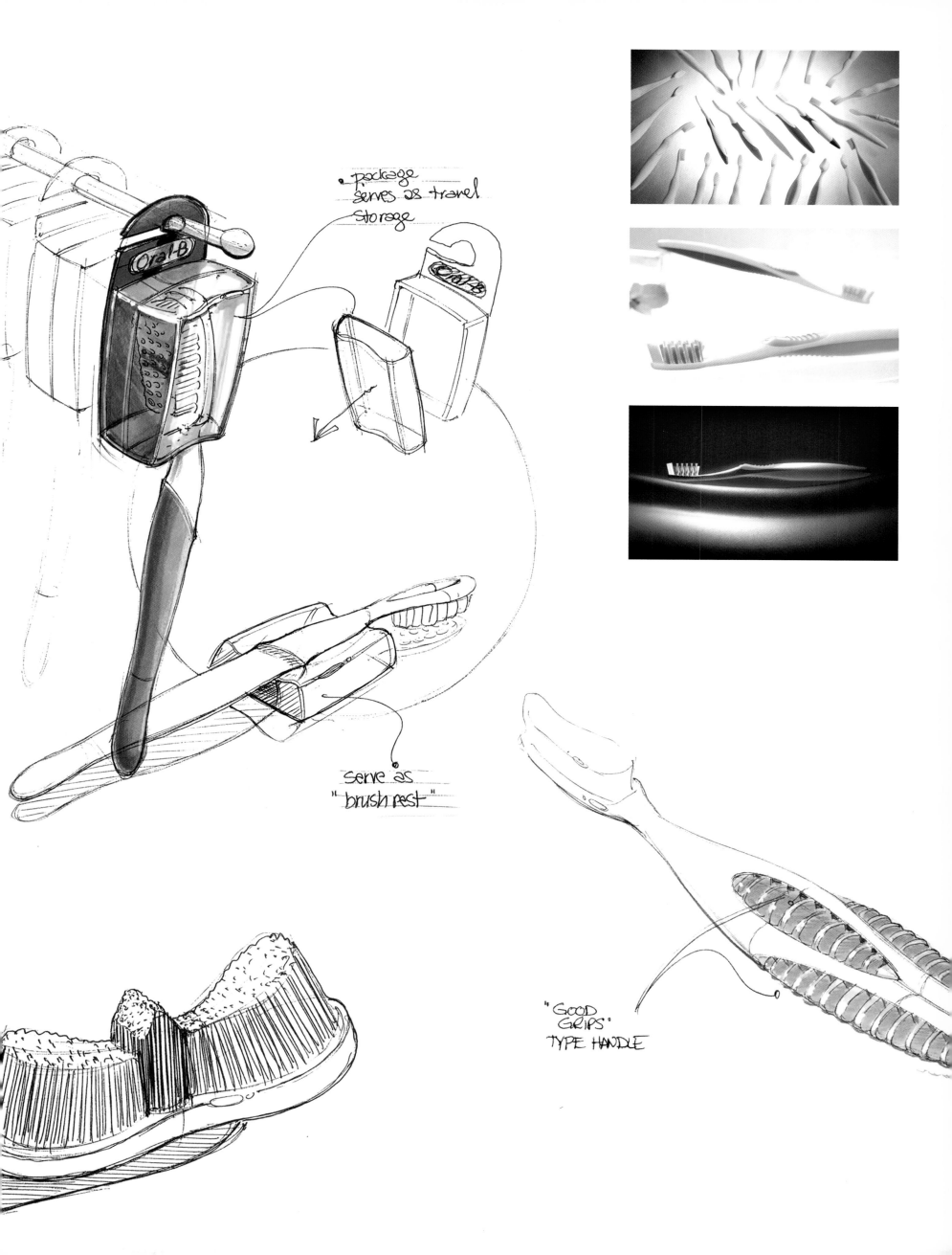

package
serves as travel
storage

Oral-B

Oral-B

serve as
"brush rest"

"GOOD
GRIPS"
TYPE HANDLE

Bottle Opener

Design
Marc Newson
Client
Alessi
1997

94

Marc Newson Ltd
Marc Newson

Dish Doctor
Drainer
Design
Marc Newson
Client
Magis
1997

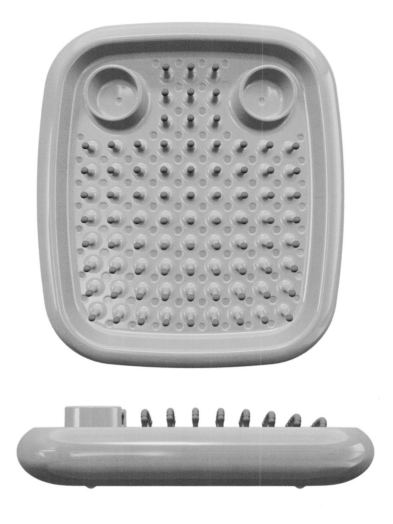

I have always been labelled as a furniture designer, although that only represents a small part of what I do. Although I consider myself a designer I don't see why people should be pigeonholed and I don't want them thinking that I only design certain things. I'm quite happy designing anything. There's not a big difference between designing the interior of an aeroplane or the interior of a restaurant, or a fashion boutique or, for that matter, a perfume bottle. Or even a bicycle. It's just designing objects.

I work closely with hi-tech and low-tech manufacturers on every aspect of manufacturing, prototyping and CAD technology. I don't employ designers. I'm not interested in employing designers. I design absolutely everything from beginning to end. I may be a kind of control freak in that respect, but I am not interested in having anything less than absolute control over what comes out of the studio.

I design things on paper; then I sit down with someone in front of a computer and we build it on screen. Before that I visualise about 95% of the thing in my head. I use computers as a tool to realise ideas. I'm not anti-team. I mean, I have a team. It's just that my part of the team effort is to design.

In terms of things that have shaped my creative personality, I think it's something to do with having had the opportunity to travel extensively, even as a child, and to experience different cultures. It's not design related. I never studied design; I went to art school and studied sculpture and jewellery. I've lived in France, Japan, South Korea and England. Since the age of about 12 I've never spent more than three years in the same place: I went to art school in Sydney, primarily because, at that stage, I couldn't think of anything else that I wanted to do.

Towel Hook

Design
Marc Newson

Client
Alessi
1997

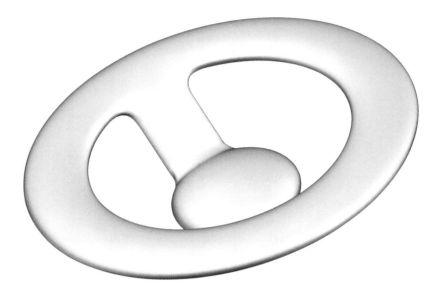

Glass Tumbler

Design
Marc Newson

Client
Iittala
1998

Art school was an absolutely fantastic place for me, because I was liberated and could do what I wanted (and I don't mean goofing off). I was completely into being there, learning how to build things and learning about sculpture. I was always interested in design, but at that time, furniture in particular. So I was able to study chairs and build them, even at art school. Historically there have been lots of artists who have played with the idea of using a chair as a kind of medium. I did these sculptural pieces which looked like chairs, just to be able to play around and build things, really.

Later I wanted to travel and I started to make pieces suitable for companies like Cappellini in Italy and Idée in Japan; things that I'd produced in limited batches by myself. The next leap was to go to Japan, not only to present illustrations or photographs of projects but the real things, which gave me that much more credibility. That was in 1987, and things really started to happen in 1988. By that stage, I had at least ten things in various degrees of production – although nothing ever exceeded 100 pieces.

Furniture's generally a low-tech industry. So moving to product design where you're working almost exclusively with different kinds of injection moulding, rapid prototyping technologies, and then moving into designing bicycles and getting into stress analysis studies, or working in the aviation industry on small jets, you start getting into really interesting territory. And that's where I'd like to be. I'm still designing for people like Alessi and Magis, but there's just so much more I want to do.

Rock
Doorstop

Design
Marc Newson

Client
Magis
1997

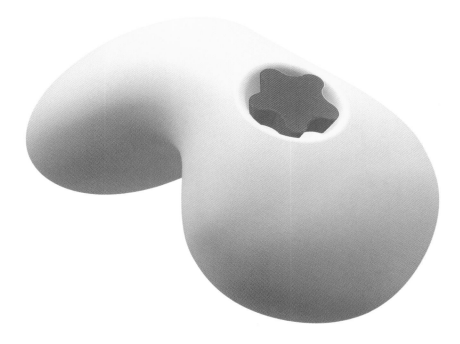

Soapdish

Design
Marc Newson

Client
Alessi
1997

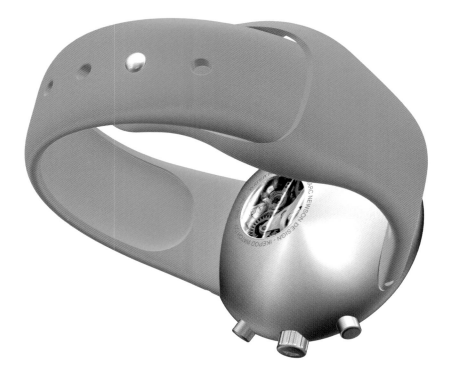

Hemipode Watch

Design
Marc Newson

Client
Ikepod
1996

Torch

Design
Marc Newson

Client
Flos
1997

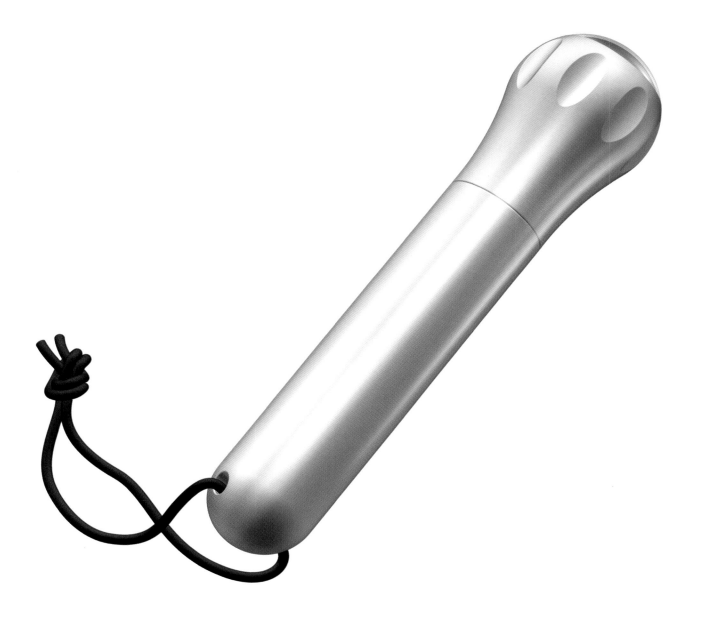

In simplistic terms my work is about form and colour, but for me it's much more about designing every aspect of the business. From the art direction, to the design, to the nitty-gritty mechanical stuff. The form and colour aspect is only 10% of the whole thing. Most of the stuff I'm preoccupied with is technical: details that people don't see. I am interested in form and colour, but I'm *more* interested in what makes things work.

I would like to have the opportunity to keep doing what I'm doing and to work on one profound project, a far-reaching project: a car, even a space station, working with NASA, perhaps. I'm very interested in science, and the relationship between science and design, and science and nature. And I think that slowly I'm heading in that direction.

I'm not particularly good at multi-tasking; I like to concentrate on one project at a time, to devote all my attention to it. I'll just think about it, until I figure it out in my head. If I'm not up to thinking about it then it just doesn't happen. It gets pushed to the end of the list. But if I'm really excited by a project then I'll give it my undivided attention.

neumeister

Neumeister Design
Alexander Neumeister

JR-W-500 Shinkansen

High-speed train

Design
Neumeister Design, Hitachi Design
Group, JR-W
Client
Hitachi
1993–1996

The design of the JR-W 500
Shinkansen is the end result of a train
project, which actually started nine
years ago, when we were approached
by Hitachi to work with them on a
design study for a high-speed train
with a maximum speed of 350km/h
(HST 350). With the HST 350, Hitachi
wanted to present a completely new
type of train to the Japanese railways.
Combining its varied technological
resources with a new, total design
approach we became part of an
international, inter-disciplinary team
of experts, freely sharing professional
know-how and expertise.

We designed the exterior and
interior of the HST 350 in close co-
operation with the Hitachi Design
Group in Tokyo, receiving technical
and research support from its
mechanical and aerodynamic
laboratories and Kasado Train Works.

The design study turned into reality
when JR-West decided to take the
exterior design as the basis for its
500 train series. Computer
simulations and aerodynamic
research led to a continuous
optimising of the front part, until the
final design was approved for
prototype construction. Today nine
train-sets of the JR West 500
Shinkansen are connecting the
central with the Southern part of
Japan.

In recognition of the exterior design,
the Imperial House of Japan awarded
Alexander Neumeister – along with
team members from Hitachi and JR
West – the Grand Prize of the
Japanese Institute of Invention and
Innovation. This was the first time a
non-Japanese received such a high
distinction for design.

Specialising – or Quality not Quantity. I started my career as industrial designer in the "let's change the
world" spirit of the late 60s studying industrial design at the Design School of Ulm, followed by a one year
scholarship at the Tokyo University of Arts in Japan. Even today, I consider this educational mix an extremely
lucky coincidence that profoundly shaped my professional working style. The school of Ulm taught me
methodological thinking, the systematic approach and somehow instilled a "feeling of responsibility" into my
work as designer. Japan taught me humility. In Japan I found objects, buildings and environments combining
materials, aesthetics and functionality together more harmoniously than I had thought possible. Even now, the
overall design quality of some traditional Japanese objects remains a quality yardstick for me that I know I will
never be able to reach.

Returning to Germany and quite innocently opening my one-man office in 1970, I decided to limit myself to
design in three areas only – transportation, medical products and electronics – because I thought these were

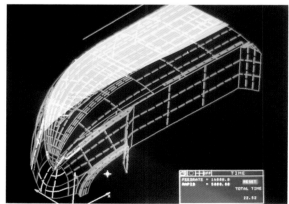

ICE 3/ICT

Trains

Design
Neumeister Design

Client
Siemens Transportation Division
1995–1998

18 years ago I started working as a designer on the development of Germany's IC-Experimental train which received the Brunel Award in 1988. As far as the exterior design is concerned, Germany's present high-speed trains, the ICE 1 and ICE 2, differ only in small details from the original ICE-V.

We recently completd the designs for the ICE 3 and ICT trains. Compared with the ICE 1 and ICE 2, these new trains have a different technical concept with all propulsion equipment placed under-floor. This has made it possible to use the whole upper part of the train as a continuous travel environment from nose point to nose point. This new technical layout, with no locomotives in front blocking the view of the passengers onto the tracks, was our basis

for an entirely new concept of the front cars. By creating a lounge directly behind the driver, future ICE/ICT passengers can experience the thrill of travelling at high speed, looking over the shoulders of the driver.

For the exterior, we purposely "linked the future with the past" – incorporating the dominant visual features of the original ICE – following the idea of optimising, instead of "differentiating by all means". Designing everything from the overall travel environment down to the smallest detail in the interior and exterior has been one of the central activities of my team and me for nearly three years. The first ICT trains are now in their testing phase while the ICE 3 trains are in full production.

These illustrations show the detailed 1:1 mock-ups in December 1995. Both industry and the railways considered it essential to see "what they were going to get" – exterior and interior with all critical details – prior to the engineering phase, in original scale and as realistically as possible.

Comparing the first conceptual sketch of ICT from our design study with the final trains which will be in operation from June 1999 on, shows how realistic our initial design proposals were and how little it was necessary to change.

The Design Process

The design process for the ICE 3/ICT trains highlights a new role for the designer – as a creator of alternatives. Design ideas were generated through a limited, international competition with Pininfarina of Italy, the US – based Design Works and Neumeister Design invited as participants.

After our submission was selected by the railway board we spent nearly nine months optimising our original competition proposal. Following the final OK by the railway board, detailed engineering started as an intense co-operation between engineers of industry, specialists of railways and us as designers – turning everything into 'reality'.

New Munich Subway
Subway for the City of Munich

Design
Neumeister Design

Client
Munich Transport Authorities
1997–1999

We are currently in the final detailing
phase for the next generation of
subway trains for Munich. Working
from the overall design of the
interior and exterior, down to the
last detail, the final design was
presented in the form of a 1:1 mock-
up. The train will be in operation
from the middle of 2000.

areas in which design could make a substantial contribution. I believed that designing the 1001st chair would be a waste of energy. Somehow this remained a core belief throughout the next 30 years.

Neumeister Design has gradually grown to its present size and structure – today it is still a relatively small group comprising six industrial designers and one model-maker, each highly professional in their areas. Additional support staff working in a recently renovated old building in the centre of Munich complete this centralgroup. Surrounding the design team is a vast network of specialists – from engineering, large-scale model-making, architecture to photography – with whom we have many years of working experience. This structure gives us both great flexibility and the ability to create the ideal mix of specialists for each project.

Early in my career I was fortunate to work with MBB (Messerschmitt Bölkow Blohm) – a company that no longer exists under this name. In the early 70s, MBB had started a "New Transportation Systems Group" looking into such diverse and speculative topics as electrically powered vans for urban use, automated transit systems or magnetic levitation trains. As the only industrial designer and fresh out of school, I was immediately confronted with highly complex projects. But most importantly, I was introduced to an open-minded atmosphere of inter-professionally composed teams of engineers and scientists of all sorts who lacked all the "anti-designer reflexes" my colleagues complain about so frequently. Therefore, inter-disciplinary teamwork became the most natural way of working together on complex projects.

I quickly discovered that I had to learn the language of my team partners if I wanted to get my message across, and that I had to understand electronics, production technology, aerodynamics or engineering in order to be able to present sound alternatives. There was no way I could withdraw into an "artistic ivory tower" if I wanted to remain an influential member of the team. We still have that working style today.

Within these teams we created nearly all the MagLev Transrapid trains and the IC Experimental train. In the same spirit we worked together with our Japanese design and engineering partners to design the JR-West 500 Shinkansen. Today we can look back at eight years of inspiring teamwork with our Hitachi partners. This experience gave us the basis for designing the next generation of Germany's high-speed trains – the ICE 3 and ICT – together with our industry partners and members of German railways.

Today we are probably better known for our work in transportation design than in medical products and

Euregia

Car Ferry

Design
Neumeister Design

Client
Bodan-Werft
1995–1996

The new car ferry Euregia connects the German city of Friedrichshafen with the Swiss city of Romanshorn on Lake Constance. Its visual concept resembles a "floating bridge" with abundant use of glass both for the car deck and the restaurant on the first floor. Starting with the overall concept we designed the whole interior and exterior – down to the smallest details.

electronics. This is largely because there too, we mostly work on the design of professional equipment or high-tech medical products such as lasers for surgery, lithotripters, heart/lung machines etc. These projects simply do not claim so much public notice as the design of a kettle or an office chair.

It goes without saying that teamwork plays a central part in our in-house working style. Over the years each of us has acquired specialist knowledge which can be shared quickly. Another characteristic feature of Neumeister Design is our dedication to detail. We strive to remain involved in a project from the conceptual phase down to the final detailed work. Only in this way can we ensure that we achieve the kind of design quality that makes the difference! Even today, we work for a relatively small number of clients – large internationally-renowned corporations, smaller innovative companies or government agencies. Most of them have been with us for many years.

My meeting in 1988 with Angela Carvalho, a Brazilian designer studying in Germany, was again one of those lucky coincidences which seem to have marked so many phases of my life. Having searched – together with Gudrun Neumeister, my former wife – for practical and effective ways to transfer design experience and know-how to Third World countries, working both in professional working groups and as vice president of ICSID, our meeting became the basis for a long partnership and friendship laying the ground for NCS Design Rio – with design studios and workshops in Rio de Janeiro. NCS today is one of the most successful design offices in Brazil working for large national and international clients such as PetroBras, Caixa Economica and Xerox. For me, these past years have increasingly become a life in two cultures – living and working in Germany and Brazil.

Looking ahead, in Germany we want to continue working in our areas of specialisation, excelling in all three of them with a particularly high design standard. At the same time we are beginning to look at these areas from a different, more comprehensive perspective – for instance, looking at ways to create travel environments with additional service components to make travel a positive experience instead of merely designing a vehicle interior or exterior.

Another new field of interest is an alternative high technology. This is a logical platform for utilising our past experience – combining high-tech elements with natural materials and basic needs to create more environmentally friendly products with a longer life expectancy and a better economical balance.

pentagram

Pentagram
Robert Brunner

Apple 20th Anniversary Mac

Design
Robert Brunner, Jonathan Ive, Danny De Iuliis, Jay Meschter

Client
Apple Computer Inc
1996

Developed while I was Design Director at Apple.

Over the course of my career, I've learned a few things. Some through success, most of them by mistake. These thoughts do not represent ideals anyone else should necessarily subscribe to; it is simply my own informal operation manual.

1. It's about content, not process. I believe process is a personal thing. It is our own way of getting to an idea, to develop it, test it and refine it. Many designers are in love with their process and in fact see it as the primary value that they provide. I will not argue that there is great joy in the journey and that the way you go about it can save time, money and pain. This is fine, I just believe that it is the content of the work that matters.

We happen to have a very basic process. We explore, develop and understand the problem. We come up with ideas, explain them, refine them, test and document them. It is fairly linear and scalable. But in the end our process is no better or worse than anyone else's, because it is the content of the final design that matters, not how we got there. If the content is there, the user will see it, touch it, experience it, understand it and hopefully, delight in it. Many times the richest idea is the first because it is so naïve. It is hard to regulate this innocence through process.

2. It's OK to screw up. It's too easy to be risk adverse. In today's business climate of speed and predictability, risk is truly a four-letter word. The problem is that risk translates directly to innovation. What happens is that as we are pressed for time and dollars, we do what we did last time since we know how and we had good results. But if we are to move forward, we must allow ourselves to fail and try something completely new. Have a back-up plan, but allow room to blow it completely. Even in absolute failures, the learning can be fantastic.

3. Always search for the truth. As noble as this sounds, it's just a way of sorting through the enormous amount of information, inputs, opinions, politics and possibilities incumbent with the development of any product. The "truth" is simply the idea of finding the right answer. The right concept, form, detail, function, cost, effort,

**Diba Information
Appliance**

TV Set-Top Box

Design
Robert Brunner,
James Toleman

Client
Diba Inc
1996

Diba Internet offers e-mail
and web access. It features an
offbeat "melon slice" unit
with a wedge-shaped case,
concave top surface and
amusing conical vents that
resemble watermelon seeds.

Diba Internet Telephone

Design
Robert Brunner,
James Toleman

Client
Diba, Inc
1996
A counter-top
Info-Appliance for e-mail,
phone and fax. The small
display shows "in basket"
when closed. Opening the
keyboard exposes the large
display.

whatever. The reason that I need to find the truth is because I am corrupt. Corrupt in that I fall in love easily and find so many ways to rationalise and sell my heart's desire. But I also feel an enormous responsibility to my patrons. So we search for the truth, walking though the problem and our solution, mentally testing the work. Asking tough questions of it. Is it really doing what it needs to do? Is it telling me the right thing? Is it good enough? Often the truth is not pleasant. But one certain truth is that if I ignore it, I usually regret it.

4. It should last. Product design can be a trendy thing. I don't really like trends. That is not to say that I am unaffected by them. It is natural to reference what surrounds you, what you see. I like new and different things, but I don't always see them being part of my existence and I don't have to like them just because they are new. When it comes to the objects that we design, I would like them to outlast whatever the "du jour" happens to be. Again, I owe it to those I work for to do so. This may have something to do with my Modernist roots, but in a less idealistic way. I look at the things happening around me, see what is challenging and extract what I feel is good and pure. If we have a use for it, we'll play with it and see where it goes. But in the end, I want to like it five years from now.

5. Context is important. I don't like designing in a vacuum. Early in my career, I was focused on art and impressing my peers. While this still drives me to some degree, I have become equally driven by the context of our work. Understanding where the design fits into someone's life, the environment, the client's business model, the competitive landscape, and the manufacturing scenario. I think you need to get outside yourself and

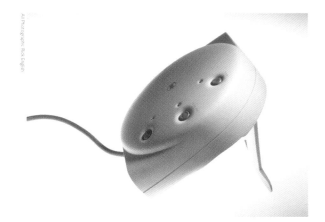

Micrus Light Source Enclosure

Design
Robert Brunner,
Benjamin Chia

Client
Micrus Corporation
1999

A piece of medical equipment used to treat brain aneurysms. The unit uses laser light to activate release of a microscopic platinum coil placed in the aneurism via a catheter; allowing the aneurism to heal.

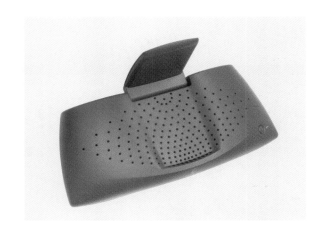

ShareWave

Set-Top-Box

Design
Robert Brunner,
Barbara Sauceda

Client
Sharewave Inc
1999

This PC enhancement product allows multiple home users to simultaneously run different applications such as games, education, home productivity, work-at-home, and internet access on a single PC from their preferred locations – wirelessly.

your studio and learn what people, society and business are all about. Appreciating all of this, yet still pushing and creating interesting things is the problem. Doing art and making it work in context is an enormous challenge. In fact, I've come to believe that anybody out of school with talent can think of exciting things. Good designers know how to build exciting things, in context.

6. My mom doesn't care. This is a metaphor for me to test relevance. My mom isn't interested in process, technology, manufacturing issues, or the subtleties of developing a form. She doesn't care about all the effort and clever thinking it took to create a design. My mom does care about the value something provides for her. Is it pretty? Is it useful? Does it work? Is it a fair price? These are the things she cares about. She doesn't care that it was easier for the project engineer to design a part a certain way, she only knows it doesn't look or feel right. So we push to do it the right way. And when we find ourselves wallowing in our own hubris about how smart we are, I just need to ask myself: "Does Mom care about this?"

7. You are only as strong as those who carry you. It doesn't matter who you are, but the quality of the people you work with defines the quality of your work. I have to trust in the creative abilities of the designers on our team. It is important that your team supports you, but that they can also challenge you, tell you when you are wrong, and can make your ideas better. Luckily, I have a great team working with me. We are a small group, culturally diverse but philosophically centered. We like to have fun. We laugh together and push each other to do better. Their talent inspires me and their enthusiasm and commitment keeps me fresh and motivated.

Typhoon

Surf Watch

Design
Robert Brunner, Chris Lenart,
Ray Riley, Gene Yanku
Benjamin Chia

Client
Nike Inc
1999

This watch provides data
on high and low tides for
175 beaches worldwide, as
well as wave conditions.
The one-piece translucent
polyurethane band is nearly
indestructible.

philips

Philips Design
Stefano Marzano

New Media, Old Walls

Philips Design
1995

It is the role of industry to suggest ways in which people can enjoy both the tremendous benefits technology offers and at the same time enhance their traditional values and experiences. It will be up to designers and manufacturers to give shape to the myriad new inter-relations which will arise between people, objects, space, time and circumstances, to bring together past, present and future in a home environment which is both highly stimulating and deeply satisfying. The challenge, they face is to reconcile technology and traditional domestic qualities, to make new objects and new media at home within old walls.

Culinary Art

Philips Design
1999

In all human societies, food is
surrounded by social and personal
rituals that are deeply embedded
in our culture. Today, the pleasures
of mealtimes can help us to
compensate for the rushed pace
and complexity of our lives. In a
recent project called Culinary
Art, a multidisciplinary team of
Philips Design, together with
experts from Philips Domestic
Appliances, took a fresh look at
the way we currently prepare, eat
and serve food, and how we may
be doing it in the near future.
Based on an analysis of lifestyle
trends, the project applies new
digital technologies to create
potential new appliances and
settings so that people can enjoy
traditional benefits and
experiences within their fuller,
faster and more varied lifestyles.
The resulting vision of future
home appliances was presented at
the 1999 Domotechnica.

I work in what is very much a "melting pot" environment. Philips Design is a real mix of cultures and disciplines. At our main studios in Holland we have about 250 designers, trend analysts, ergonomists, psychologists, anthropologists and other specialists. At our branches around the world we have another 200. They come from more than 30 different countries, and the average age is under 30, so it's a pretty lively atmosphere and reflects our interest in the richness and diversity of cultures around the world. The design of our main studio is very open, too, though there are 'little houses' for meeting places and quiet work.

My personal office is also a melting pot. I'm surrounded by books, models, product concepts, mementoes and things that just interest me, from all over the world.

I strongly believe in a "polyglot" approach to design. We focus on the relationship between people and their natural and human-made environment, and we try to enhance that relationship through the products we design. In doing so, we obviously have to deal with global culture, but local cultures are the ultimate source of diversity. So we try to 'be everywhere' so that we can understand both the global and the local. That's what I mean when I say our approach is polyglot. It's also polychrome, polyform. Poly-everything, in fact.

What is product design? I usually say it's two things: an act of love and a political statement. It's an act of love because you have to do it with absolute love for people and things. Design, after all, is about relationships, about harmony. And it's a political statement because your designs are clear proposals for the direction society should take. What you create is your suggestion as to how life should be lived in the future.

I was born in Italy, near Milan, the son of a typographer and an actress. But I was greatly influenced by my grandfather, who was a tailor. I spent a lot of time as a child with him in his workshop, playing with the wooden

moulds and forms he used, learning about cloth, observing how my grandfather helped his customers decide what they wanted, and how he built up a relationship of trust and loyalty with them. Now I realise I was learning about the power of aesthetics and communication. I also saw how he didn't just limit himself to making clothes. He advised his customers on the 'whole picture' and took great care in the whole process from start to finish, including advising people how to stand, how to behave; in other words, how to look their best in the clothes he had made for them. He was the director of a show that starred his customers. And of course, I also saw him tidying up and doing the accounts after closing time, so I knew there was a lot of 'behind the scenes' work as well.

When I was a bit older, I lived in a very cosmopolitan environment with many friends from other countries, and I think it was visiting their homes and talking with them and their families that really aroused my interest in different cultures. Later on, I worked with Dutch and American companies, and now I live in Holland and travel a lot. But I'm still very much Italian at heart.

The people who have influenced me most haven't been big names, particularly; just friends I've met along the way, especially those with a philosophical turn of mind who were interested in tossing ideas around. I'm not a follower of a particular school or movement: I'd call myself an eclectic. A defender of opportunities for improvement, for pluralism, diversity, the richness of life. Not in a purely visual or aesthetic sense, in terms of style, but rather in the sense of achieving perfect harmony. An evening with friends, for instance, when everything is just right – the right time, the right place, the right people, the right food. Everything. Perfect harmony and balance.

Plugged Furniture

Philips Design
1997

At the end of the 20th century, we find ourselves in a period of unprecedented technological change. It affects all aspects of our lives. But it is, perhaps, in the home that we will be touched most deeply. Much more than the home of today, with its telephone, television and washing machine, the home of tomorrow will rely on technology. Although the new technology, like the old, is intended to improve the quality of life, how can we make sure that it will? Home is supposed to be a place where we live according to our own values, where we can be ourselves. But if complex technology invades this space, will people come to resent it? The task of integrating technology into the traditional home setting is one which will grow in scope and complexity in the coming decades. The pace at which technology enters the home can only accelerate. Plugged Furniture is the result of a collaboration between Philips and Leolux. It offers three products: Ironie, Tavoli and Parete – their response to the challenge of helping people make technology part of their domestic lives in a more complete way than ever before.

Television at the Crossroads

Philips Design
1994

Where is television heading? Where will this leave us, as viewers? With technologies merging to create new multimedia possibilities and the information superhighway coming ever closer, television is about to embark on an exciting new phase in its history, one that will affect our lives even more deeply than it has already. High time, then, that we all gave some thought to what this will mean for our domestic and working lives, our social structures and our psychological well-being. Based on an innovative series of design workshops held in Italy and Holland, Television at the Crossroads presents a collection of essays and design concepts that address precisely these issues. Television at the Crossroads will be especially stimulating for those interested in design, social trends, and the new media. But the ideas and concepts it contains are guaranteed to make any viewer look at 'that box in the corner' with new eyes.

I'm a great admirer of Fellini's films. I particularly appreciate the meaningful aesthetic of his filmic language, especially the way he deals with grand themes and at the same time manages to express them in small details. You get the micro and macro at the same time, as it were. In a sense, that's what I try to do in my design work, trying to understand the big picture of human needs and desires and interpret them on the level of individual products or features.

I suppose one of our most well-known projects of recent years has been the Philips-Alessi line of kitchen appliances. I think I can claim we were the first to bring "design" back into electrical kitchen appliances. It was the result of a research-based approach that we've since extended to a wide range of other products. The way I tackle a problem is not to try and solve it immediately. That often results in a quick fix that doesn't last. Instead, I try to establish an intellectual and emotional sense of trust and sharing with the client, building a partnership, identifying, adapting and developing capabilities I can offer to help add value to the client's business. The first task is to define the problem clearly. It often reminds me of my grandfather. He didn't just say, "OK, you want a new suit: I'll make you one." He would always find out more about the occasions on which it would be worn, who else would be there, what sort of impression the customer wanted to make on whom, and so on. Looking back, it was all about determining the right positioning for the customer, about getting to the root of the problem first and only then trying to provide a solution.

We took this approach when tackling the problem of repositioning Philips several years ago. The aim was to translate Philips' technological superiority into ways of making a positive contribution to the quality of people's lives. But the basic problem was: what "quality of people's lives" should we be addressing? What sort of

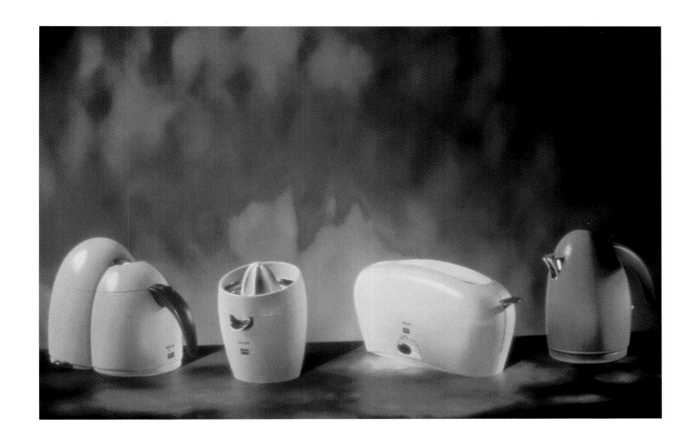

Rehumanising the kitchen, restoring the balance between speed, hygiene and high-end convenience on the one hand, and human warmth, repose and social ritual on the other, has come to fruition in the Philips-Alessi Line. The products – a toaster, a kettle, a coffee-maker and a citrus press – have a distinctive round, friendly form, evoking memories, emotional involvement and intimacy. Their colours, neither intrusively strong nor insipidly weak, suggest maturity. Their stable appearance and sturdy, high-quality materials convey a sense of reliability. Easy-to-use and easy-to-clean, but without sacrificing the essential 'human touch and feel', these products bring a new domestic quality to kitchen appliances. The Philips-Alessi Line products are not only tools which work well and are pleasing to use. They also convey cultural values of elegance and humanity – aesthetic and poetic qualities that help the owner express something of his or her own individuality. We are used to seeing this in clothing, furnishing and even automobiles. The Philips-Alessi Line breaks new ground in extending it into the kitchen, reflecting the current revival of interest in culinary art and gastronomic ritual. Kitchen appliances are no longer hardware – they have become humanware.

products do people see as improving the quality of their lives? To answer this question, we set up a research programme called Vision of the Future. This led to a wide range of concepts for possible future products that would serve as triggers for debate, both within Philips and outside, among opinion-leaders and in the media. It produced a lot of feedback that has served as input for strategic planning and the development of Philips' new positioning. I think this type of approach illustrates the distinction between being merely a supplier and being an intelligent partner. Of course, this partnership approach, with its strong element of sharing, has been relatively easy to establish within the Philips Company, since we all share the same ultimate goals. But even for clients outside the company, this is the approach we take whenever possible.

What I see as becoming increasingly significant in the near future is the development of 'ambient intelligence' – artificial intelligence (in the form of computing power and sensors) entering into everything around us. At the same time, the technology gap between companies will get smaller, and we'll find that the real competitive edge will lie not so much in technological superiority, as in the past, but in the form given to that shared technology. Technology will in large measure become invisible. That is, it will be incorporated into the parts of our environment that are so embedded in our cultures that we can't do without them, such as walls, furniture or clothes. So the home of tomorrow will actually look more like the home of yesterday than the home of today. To the extent that technology doesn't become entirely invisible, it will take on interesting and colourful forms: people will use it (as they sometimes do now) to express something of themselves. Tomorrow's human-made environment will not be full of grey boxes like those of today but be a world of 'butterflies and flowers'.

priestman goode

Priestman Goode
Paul Priestman

Hot Spring

Radiator

Design
Paul Priestman

Manufacturer
Bisque Ltd
1997

Hot Spring is a complete amalgamation of manufacturing principals, product performance and design aesthetic. There is not one part of the design that is not vitally important or superfluous to the whole. Two-metre tall version is pictured here.

Shopper

Shopping Trolley

Design
Priestman Goode

Client
Marks & Spencer
1997

A speedy, compact shopping trolley.

We are beginning to live in a world of virtual products. The old adage concerning function and form is being left behind as "the product offer" becomes number one, and everything else follows: on-line music, virtual shopping, 24-hour banking. Many electronic products are being marginalised into unseen entities with no tangible bearing on our everyday lives. What a result! The product designer's role now spans from inception to production.

I work with my business partner Nigel Goode in the centre of London's West End. Hearts of cities buzz. Fifteen designers from around the world, many who have studied at the Royal College of Art in London, work in a barn-like open-plan space where two industrial buildings have been opened into one. Behind this 19th century exterior there is music, pivoting glass partitions, spanner door handles. Racks of pushbikes hang from the walls, with staff scooters parked outside. In the foam room anything from full-size train mock-ups to the tiniest digital cameras are produced in tandem.

As a studio we consciously strive to work on a wide range of products so we don't become specialised in any one area. We believe diversity of work is crucial to staying fresh in our thinking. Through this we all keep learning, ideas and processes can cross-fertilise between industries, life is more interesting and clients receive that little extra. At any one point, my partner, Nigel Goode, and I may be working with a team of designers on anything from aircraft interiors, to trains and lighting. To create products we work with a village of specialists and bring together teams, as the projects require.

Upstream and downstream is the way we are now working with many clients. Going upstream involves working more and more with them on the conception of products, their reason and functionality. In some instances, we become involved before a new product project has even been decided upon. A prime example of this is a range of mobile communicators we have been developing for Orange, the mobile telecommunications

Mobile Video Phones

Design
Priestman Goode

Client
Orange
1998

The soft-moulded 'Futurephone' is aimed at social use. It slips easily into a pocket and can be flipped open with one hand to reveal its two touch sensitive screens.

Mobile Video Phones

Design
Priestman Goode

Client
Orange
1998

The 'Videophone' has the feel, familiarity and protocol of a paperback book but provides full colour video-conferencing, fax-viewing, video mailbox, e-mail and interactive television – all whilst on the move.

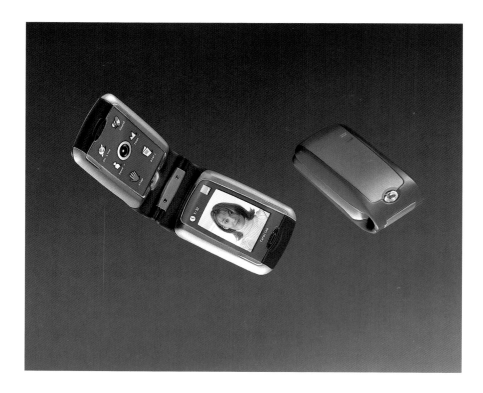

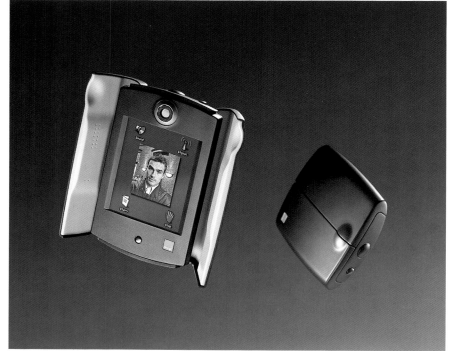

120 provider. Many of the projects we work on now don't necessarily end up as tangible products, because in many instances products are becoming less prominent. The result may be a service rather than a product as the product offer takes the lead.

We have also been moving downstream to an area we have termed "manufacture management". In early 1998, Nigel, myself and our senior designers set up the manufacturing management company called Plant, also based in London. In its first year Plant is busy producing five products around the world. Plant is, in effect, an extension of our design process; good products are mainly due to good management.

We are extremely pro-active, continually innovating our products and ourselves. To do this we bring together teams of specialists relevant to our decided project. These specialists include electronic designers, software designers, ergonomists, colourists, interface designers and so on. This is a far cry from the concept of a crazy inventor fiddling reclusively with madcap ideas. We run a well-managed directional team all working closely together. What interests us is high volume, mass-produced products that touch the lives of as many people as possible. The proof of a good product is whether it is successful in the market it has been designed for.

For me a germ of an idea comes from an inkling of a need. I think about the parameters and the thought process and then mull it over, often for months and months. Some ideas never get past an interesting thought and go out with the tide along the coastline, where I spend much of my time relaxing. Some ideas make it to the foam room or workshop but even fewer make it any further. One of our best-known products, the Hot Spring radiator, was an exception.

The Hot Spring radiators came about from a lunch with Geoffrey Ward, founder of the UK-based radiator specialists, Bisque. It started with a clear thought and then a napkin scribble, a year later it was still being developed and perfected. The simplest ideas are always the most difficult. When a traditional tubular radiator

Virgin Trains

Product Design
Priestman Goode

Graphic Design
Start

Interior Design
JHL

Client
Virgin Rail Group
1999

Computer development
images of the new Virgin Rail
high-speed tilting trains for
the UK rail network.

is manufactured, each intersection of tube has to be welded and finished which is labour intensive and costly. The Hot Spring radiator is manufactured by coiling a continual length of tube, avoiding much of the costs associated with radiator manufacture. The whole radiator is made rigid by the return pipe which is attached at key points to the coil; this also neatly forms the fixing area for mounting to the wall. Hot Spring is a complete amalgamation of manufacturing principles, production performance and design aesthetics, there is not one part of the design that is not vitally important or superfluous to the whole. Now in its third year of manufacture, and sales growing steadily around the world, the design is beginning to show that it has longevity.

In that sense, product design at its best is a seamless process of product design and aesthetics. What I find fascinating and what I am continually looking for in my work is the creation of the unquantifiable aspect in a design that differentiates a product from being just another to a "must have". That element cannot be an add-on, it has to be crucial to the design, synonymous with the whole. Often it does not cost any more to produce, but requires a lot of thinking time. I have always enjoyed it when people ask about Hot Spring: "Was it designed? I thought it just happened"!

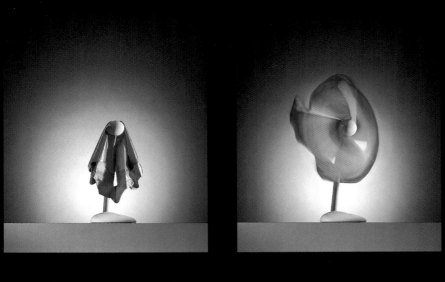

Soft Fan

Concept

Design
Priestman Goode
1996

Inspiration came from sailing craft, physical principals of air pressure and centrifugal force. As the fan has no dangerous moving parts it requires no bulky protective guard. When switched off the fabric assembly folds to a fraction of its size. When dirty it can be washed in a machine. The form and finish of the hard parts are reminiscent of pebbles on a beach.

Instant Print Camera

Design
Priestman Goode

Client
Fisher Price
1997

Instant print digital camera
for kids.

Digital Camera

Design
Priestman Goode

Manufacturer
Vision

Client
Rockwell and Vision
1998

A tiny, high quality digital
video camera.

Vision USB

Video Camera

Design
Priestman Goode

Client
Vision
1998

Video camera
for use with a PC.

Clio
Renault
1997

"The small car with big car
refinement."

renault

Renault
Patrick Le Quément

Photograph Patrick Surédon

Espace, Scenic, Twingo

Monospace Models
Renault
1996

Renault is the first – and still
the only – manufacturer to
offer a whole range of
monospaces.

Clio

Renault
1997

"The small car with big car
refinement."

I attach a great deal of importance to my working environment. When I arrived at Renault in 1987, I was placed in premises devoid of any charm whatsoever. Not only were they depressingly boring and uninspiring, they had the added attraction of being far too small. This was a plus point in some ways, because a request for a move was more than justified. We then managed to take over 20,000 square metres in an old abandoned factory down by the Seine for our operations: the same place where Louis Renault had set up the company back in 1898. What we ended up with may have been out of step with the rest of the company, but it soon became the must-see area within Renault: a real cultural hot spot.

It was at that time I took on an interior designer to help out with our professional surroundings, including what my own office should look like. Then, in 1997, we decamped to set up shop to the west of Paris, at a place called Guyancourt. Here, Renault has built a vast complex – the Technocentre – to house all the creative teams and units of the company, able to accommodate 8,000 people, including the 270 that make up the design team. The Renault plant down by the Seine was like a town within a town. The Technocentre is rather like that too, but this time like a completely new town, in its own greenfield site. The key advantage of the Technocentre is that it enables our small team to rub shoulders and – one could say brains – on a day-to-day basis with literally thousands of colleagues beavering away in product and process engineering, purchasing, and so on.

The first thing I require from a manufactured product is that it delivers the service expected of it, and that it does this in a reliable and enduring manner; that it delivers the promises the manufacturer makes to the customer. Apart from this what attracts me in general to a manufactured article? Two things really. First of all, is it intelligent as an object? This intelligence might be expressed in the form of a useful innovation, or an indication as to how the object operates. I once read a description of the French set down by an English writer. He wrote that the French worship the cult of intelligence, that they love to shine intellectually, and that this

Scenic Production Car

Renault
1996

The Scenic (production car) is a direct descendant of the concept car bearing the same name: a transport solution that has proved "right first time".

Scenic Concept Car

Renault
1991

Scenic Concept Car

Renault
1991

The most important part of this exercise was not the exterior styling, as most journalists thought, but the interior.

126 makes them all the more annoying as they don't seem to be any more intelligent than their Spanish, Bulgarian or Belgian neighbours. I completely agree with this, adding that this major failing and legendary light-hearted attitude of the French is not without its appeal, as can be seen in the Eiffel Tower, the 2CV or the Twingo. The other thing I want from an industrial product is excellent perceived quality which conveys the impression of a well thought out design and a complete control of the manufacturing process itself.

A major influence on my career as a designer has been the fact that France and I have been on bad terms for quite a long period of time. I loved France, and would have liked to spend all my time there, but I couldn't find any opportunities for work that bettered what was on the table for me in England or Germany. A major advantage of this absence, which lasted 19 years, was that I never stopped musing on the question of what Frenchness in industrial design actually meant. It's like the story of the chap strolling along the water's edge, who spots a fish drifting along with the current. It's a nice sunny day and the man would really like to take a dip. What's the water like? he asks the fish. What water would that be? the fish replies. I am like a fish that life's circumstances have taken out of its native waters. This enforced distance between myself and my homeland has shown me that the water does indeed exist, it has helped me to see France's distinct cultural differences, to have a clearer focus on its strong points as well as its weak points. I drew immense pleasure from reading Daniel Jones and James Womack's book, *The Future of the Automobile*, when I realised that I was not the only one in Europe to ponder on the interest that the different EU states would have in exploiting their specific cultural traits through their industrial output.

As far as auto design is concerned, it is a widely-recognised fact that Renault is a pioneering and innovative manufacturer. This can be seen in our current range in the form of the Espace, the Twingo, the Scenic, and the new Kangoo – not to mention our concept cars. But less is made of the firm's perseverance from the outset –

Twingo

Renault
1992

Twingo was conceived from the inside out. Much copied since its launch, yet never equalled. Just like the Mini, the Twingo possesses a "perfect" design feature: the four wheels at the four corners of the body.

Kangoo

Renault
1997

Kangoo, continuing the practical tradition of the R4.

Espace Interior

Renault
1996

The heating unit has been moved from the centre of the dashboard to make way for a huge storage bin.

some might say its stubbornness – in its functionalist approach to car design, an approach that has known great success as well as failure. I'm thinking now of the R16, launched in 1965, the first top-of-the-range saloon on the market boasting a rear hatch and a modular rear seat design. Result: highly successful. Then, in 1975, along came the R30. Result: a failure and a rather painful one at that. Next, the R25 of 1985, again at the top end of the range: 50% successful. And now the Safrane today. In the meantime Renault launched the Espace.

If an automaker could be a sportsperson, Renault would be a boxer, a rugby player. You have to know when to go on the attack, but also be able to go with the flow, take the punches, that's all part of the game too. In spite of its history, the following question was posed: shouldn't Renault pull out of making hatchbacks, of the R25 and Safrane variety, and focus instead on totally revolutionary designs like the Espace? I approached my principal client, appealing to his love and respect for tradition. The word came back that we could persevere in our perseverance! We then brought out the Initiale concept car, followed by a second one, the Vel Satis, to make it clear we would not be abandoning the luxury, functional saloon segment. And that principal client? None other than Renault's Chairman, Louis Schweitzer.

A major consideration that occupies our every working day is the globalisation of the economy in general and its effect on manufacturing and sales within the auto industry in particular. Will such changes, as a matter of course, take us towards "global" products and lead us in the direction of a "world car"? This question is in fact, not a new one. I remember the same thing back in the mid-70s, when I was still at Ford... and my conviction remains unchanged: paradoxically, despite the globalisation of our industry, more and more people will be wanting innovative models. The trick, as far as the manufacturers are concerned, will be about being able to speed up design and manufacturing times. So, I'll leave you with two key words for the future: innovation and speed.

Vel Satis

Renault
1998

A luxury coupé created to
celebrate Renault's centenary.

Initiale Concept Car

Renault
1995

The Initiale Concept Car,
or "how to be top-of-the-
range without being English,
German or Italian, but
French". The driving position
is a lesson in Zen
management of simplexity.

Photograph: Peter Vann

Photograph: Gilles Bouquillon

B.O.O.P. Low Table

Design
Ron Arad

Client
Gallery Mourmans
1998

Mirror polished, inflated
superplastic aluminium.

arad

Ron Arad & Associates
Ron Arad

B.O.O.P. Coffee Table

Design
Ron Arad

Client
Gallery Mourmans
1998

Mirror polished, inflated
superplastic aluminium.

B.O.O.P. Low Table

Design
Ron Arad

Client
Gallery Mourmans
1998

Mirror polished, inflated
superplastic aluminium.

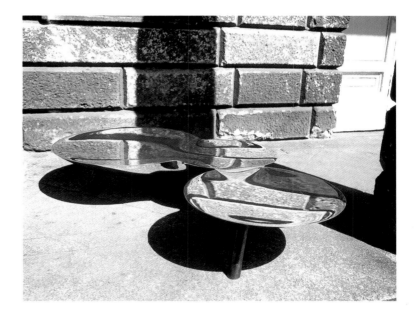

In the early 80s, while doing Rover chairs and concrete stereos, Vitra International (Who? A Swiss company? They produce Eames for Europe?) commissioned me to design a piece for the "Vitra Editions", along with Sottsass, Pesce, Kuramata (I knew who they were) – and I blew it. But I came up with what is still one of my favourite chairs – the Well Tempered Chair. So why do I say I blew it?

Well, Vitra, in an attempt to relieve me of my ignorance about them, flew me to Basel to visit their factory and prototyping workshops. There I saw people mass produce sophisticated pieces of furniture, using state-of-the-art machinery and materials. I was also shown the biggest ever collection of chairs, complete with the Rover chair (there was no Vitra Design Museum at that time)! They also had a very impressive basement where chairs were tested to destruction, hit a million times with heavy weights, dragged by chains across the floor, set alight and other imaginative stuff. Now, they said, go back to London and design something for us. My first ever commission – and I blew it.

Instead of rising to the occasion, designing using scientist engineers, Swiss clock technology and advanced materials – all I could come up with was something I could build myself in my bucket and spade workshop: a chair made of four pieces of tempered stainless steel, bent and fastened by wing nuts, an effortless portrait of a club chair. Sitting on it was more like sitting on a waterbed than sitting on steel. Its supple flexibility would make a mockery of the chair torture contraptions in Basel – it was more like a Tom and Jerry cartoon.

B.O.O.P.
Large Floor Vase

Design
Ron Arad

Client
Gallery Mourmans
1998

Mirror polished, inflated
superplastic aluminium.

R.T.W.

Design
Ron Arad

Client
Ron Arad Associates
1997

A series of free-spinning
wheels in various sizes. The
shelves locked within the
wheel always remain level
with the floor while the outer
wheel can be rolled at will.

This Mortal Coil

Free Standing Book Case

Design
Ron Arad

Client
Ron Arad Associates
1993

Mirror polished stainless
steel strip coiled to form a
spiral. Form retained by
partitions through riveted
hinges. The hinges allow the
coil to move in a sprung
action.

132

Vitra (I certainly know who they are now!) launched my latest chair for them – the Tom Vac – in Milan in April 1999. The Tom Vac is very industrial, virtually conceived in the computer and mass-produced in their mighty clockwork factory. By the way, I don't see any distinction between furniture and product design. To me, a chair is a product – something that is made from the material to perform certain tasks. People talk about insurance policies as the product. My view is that if you are a designer you can design anything.

Since we closed our workshop in London and moved production to Italy, our studio was, for a period, crowded with drawing boards. Boards were soon replaced by screens and keyboards and we were inventing industrial products for the leading Italian design companies and dreaming up architecture. I say inventing because we are not at all interested in styling. Genuine newness is at the base of every project we work on – indeed, most of our projects are initiated rather than briefed. I have written before about my unjustified aversion to convention and I won't try to justify it now.

Do I miss having a workshop? No, not at all. Those days were exciting, fun. The workshop (laboratory), provided a playground for our ideas without having to consider practical constraints, giving us a great freedom. But after some 15 years of that, not having a workshop somehow provides an even greater freedom. With the astonishing advances in communication and I.T. technologies the world has become our workshop.

I spent the last three weeks in a studio in Holloway, making a coloured resin version of the Big Easy chair by hand so my fingernails are dirty. I thoroughly enjoyed it ... so what was I saying?

Tom-Vac

Design
Ron Arad

Client
Ron Arad Associates
1997

Vacuum formed, mirror polished, aluminium stacking chair. Stainless steel frame.

Un-Cut

Chair

Design
Ron Arad

Client
Ron Arad Associates
1997

A low, untrimmed version of the aluminium vacuum-formed Tom Vac chair. Anodised in various colours. Polished stainless steel frame. Limited edition of 50 pieces.

Fantastic Plastic Elastic

Design
Ron Arad

Client
Kartell
1998

Double-barrel aluminium extrusion frame. Transparent plastic seat. A pre-production version hasbeen used in the Ron Arad-designed Adidas Sport Cafés in France.

135

seymour powell

Seymour Powell
Richard Seymour and Dick Powell

Nexus
Internal Design Study
Motorcycle

Design
Seymour Powell
1992

The Nexus Motorcycle is an exercise in 'inversion'. Most vehicle manufacturers are trapped in the 'more weight therefore more power' conundrum, which makes fuel economy a punishing brief for the powertrain engineer. The lighter the vehicle, the less power you need and Nexus uses advanced bicycle technology to achieve this. The result is a 20kg motorcycle that only needs 3 hp to propel the user at speeds up to 45 mph. Early investigations into power technologies suggested that Nexus could run effectively on butane, rather than petrol, which could mean refuelling at a tobacconist, rather than a petrol station.

Avanti
Toaster

Design
Seymour Powell

Client
Tefal
1997

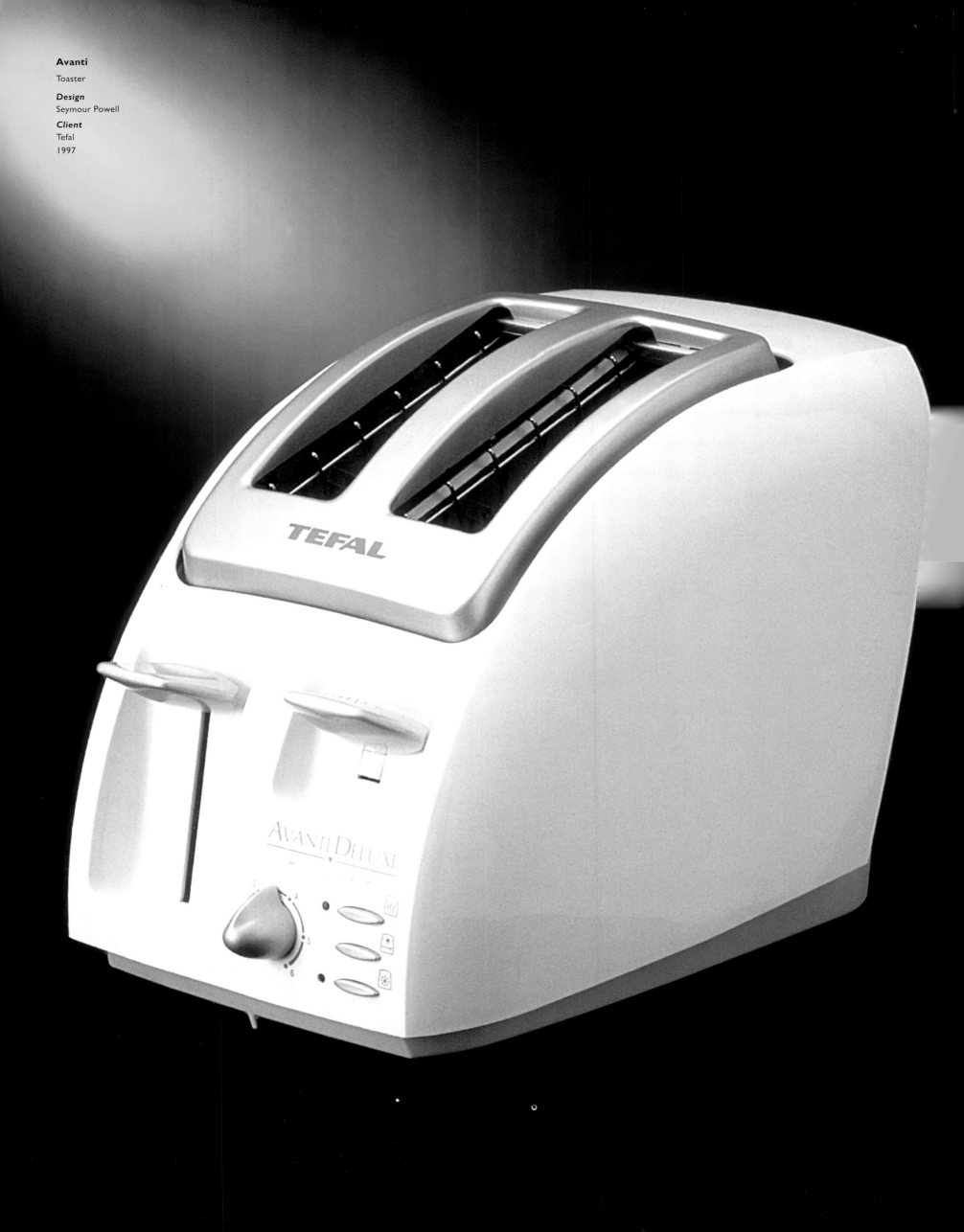

Zero Knives

Internal Design Study

Design
Seymour Powell
1998

These kitchen knives emanate from a punch-up between ourselves and an un-named client, who persisted in dumbing-down a new product to the point where it just resembled everything else on the market. Although he insisted at the outset that the new knives should be 'exciting and emotionally satisfying', his actions during the design selection process suggested that he actually wanted something that was a riskless synthesis of competitors products (a very common ailment amongst marketing managers). The design shown here is one we created from Zirconium ceramic (an artificial diamond effectively) and a carbon-fibre loaded engineering polymer. Hefts like a rapier, cuts like a laser. Not a technology statement, even though it's stuffed to the gunwales with it.

Ideal Standard Bath

Design
Seymour Powell
Client
Ideal Standard
1998

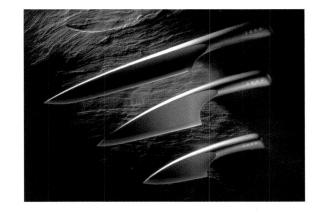

We formed the company, Seymour Powell, in the first place to give us both a firm platform from which to professionalise our vocation. Anybody who believes that design is just a job is probably in the wrong business... design is our passion, our cause and our life. Successful design partnerships are few and far between. The act of creating "uniqueness" is very much bound up with the individual ego, so much so that the very process of building certainty into one's personal "logic of creation" tends to act as a powerful corrosive on the bonds between creative partners. The one thing that has saved us is the fact that we are so very different. Although we have a very similar sense of what is good, attractive and appropriate, we come at our design solutions from totally different directions... and meet in the middle, like the two axis of a computer plotter. In that respect, we're not competing with one another, but collaborating. If you trust and respect the abilities of the other, even though they may differ dramatically to your own, then it's possible to maintain a vivid, living symbiosis.

Seymour Powell has been through several forms over the last 16 years, each one a reflection of the design team that existed at the time. In the first three or four years, the team was tiny and very young. Our output was rich in attitude and challenge, with many concept pieces being generated to demonstrate our thesis in the absence of much real work. Examples such as the powered bicycle wheel (concept for General Electric Plastics in Holland) and the electric guitar (created to provoke Vox into producing guitars that weren't just copies of other famous brands) came straight from our own pens into appearance models... they had to really, because nobody would believe the ideas unless they had the authenticity of physical presence.

Our initial work attracted a lot of attention from the media, and phase one of our development; the "boost" phase if you like, culminated in a detailed profile in "Domus" magazine, the Italian design and architecture review. Now that we were on the map in Europe, it was time for us to develop our activities farther afield. Phase two consisted of enlarging the company from a minute "hit squad", to a respectable organisation, with a clutch of blue-chip international clients to go with it. Companies such as Tefal, Norton, Philips, Casio and Clairol Appliances formed the core of our activities, whilst existing clients, such as Yamaha, extended their involvement with us. We were able to bring our imagination to bear on exciting projects, such as the high-performance motorcycle for Norton, the creation of the world's first cordless kettle for Tefal and the development of new wristwatch directions for Casio in Japan.

Whilst doing this, we continued to experiment with our own new concepts. The range of high-tech, ceramic kitchen knives grew out of the frustrated collision of views between us and one of our kitchenware clients. The

MZ Skorpion

Motorbike

Design
Seymour Powell

Client
MuZ
1993

Gep Bike Wheel

Internal Design Study

Design
Seymour Powell
1984

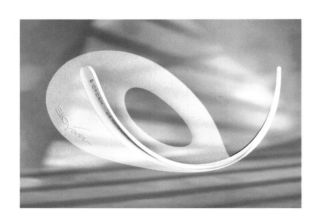

Bioform

Design
Seymour Powell

Client
Charnos
1998

The BioForm, (a completely new way of making bras), is a prosthesis which is stitched into the bra as it is made. The initial idea came from studying how the sports shoe industry has gone about developing high-tech running shoes. It replaces a dozen or so bits of fibre and cloth and creates a foundation which is comfortable, machine-washable and 'form enhancing' at the same time. It represents a complete, ground-up shift in design for a product which users have grown to put up with, rather than to love. The design project formed the subject of a television programme, 'Designs on Your...', which screened in the UK in 1998.

Baby Gs

Watches

Design
Seymour Powell

Client
Casio
1995

Nexus, an ultra-light motorcycle created by approaching the problem of individual mobility from the perspective of lightness not performance, established a benchmark of "paradigm shifting" within an industry obsessed with ever-growing weight and performance factors.

Fundamentally, our work continued along the same basic tenets: making things better, for *people*. It was at this time that we began to look long and hard at the nature of function, style and "appeal psychology" within the context of product design. It was clear to us that form didn't merely follow function, but that form is function; furnishing the user with data about the product's identity, role and operating method with a burst of "telemetry" which acted directly on the "pre-cognitive" or subconscious strata of the brain. We began to understand instinct as a reliable and potent enzyme in the creative process and started to propagate these thoughts through the media. Seymour Powell became the X-Factory... a company dedicated to improving the design of everyday objects by giving them relevance, superior performance and visceral appeal.

As we developed our international business, especially in the Far East, Seymour Powell grew once more to the size that it is today, with 20 designers and creative staff, plus the addition of SP Forecasting... a future-gazing strategy unit headed by Professor James Woudhuysen. Even now, we still spend most of our time pen (or mouse) in hand. We are, after all, still designers. The team is now headed by three Principal Designers, each with very particular skills and characteristics, and each with the same feisty individualism that we built the company on. Our portfolio now spans the entire firmament of product sectors, from automotive, marine and aviation products to domestic appliances and personal products such as cameras and watches. We still, however, persist in retaining only one operating base: our London office. We believe, rightly or wrongly, that Seymour Powell isn't a template that you can clone from, it's a living entity that takes its approach directly from its active practitioners. With clients such as Nokia, Renault and Hewlett Packard, we are helping to develop strategies for products well into a new millennium.

Naming the as yet un-named. Pulling new technologies towards the user, rather than shoving them at people relentlessly. Finding ways to help create a more sustainable future, whilst making the day pass in a more enjoyable and satisfying way... Product Design is a commercial act. It's not art. It's not sculpture. It's not about just moving the deckchairs around to create a different effect. It's about finding the unexpected, relevant solution... and having a great time in the process. The day this all becomes just a job is the day we'll jack it in.

There is much debate in the UK at present about whether design is about "styling" or about making things work better. Stupid question, really. There is no excuse for designing things that work worse than the things they replace. But worse, just like better, is a subjective issue. Worse for whom? If a vacuum cleaner uses more electricity to clean a carpet better, is that worse or better? If it costs more to manufacture a car that lasts twice as long, is that worse or better? If you design a product that is more attractive than its competitor, but works less well, have you committed a mortal sin? Well, if you have, then many contemporary designers are staring their maker in the face right now. The style versus performance debate is as fatuous as it is ill informed. If a designer begins his task with anything other than the users' needs (physical and emotional) firmly in view, then he is sinning, in our book. Is Starck's lemon squeezer a malfunctional piece of sculpture? Should a chair be the ultimate "sitting machine", or a piece of decorative art? Is a pocketable "pen" that enables diabetics to conveniently and discreetly inject themselves bad design because it costs more to make than a hypodermic syringe? Is a video recorder which looks nice, but which still can't be programmed easily after 25 years in the marketplace, good design or a crime against society? You answer these questions. But before you do, look carefully at the products you have filled your life with, and consider why you made the choices you did. Does that fancy metal toaster really make better toast? Or did you buy it to enhance your kitchen? Be honest.

Design, in our book, is the act of making things better for people. That means making them work and look better. The trick, as it always has been, is in the balance.

Lama (prototype)
Scooter

Design
Philippe Starck
Manufacturer
Aprilia
1992

starck

Starck

Phillippe Starck

Plywood Car (project)

Design
Philippe Starck
1996

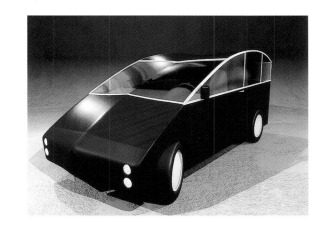

Moto X Ray Prototype

Motorbike

Design
Philippe Starck
Manufacturer
Aprilia
1996

Raymond Loewy, one of the fathers of design, came up with a slogan in the 50s that brought him fame 143
and had a major impact on the growth of the design profession: "ugliness does not sell". At that time, he was probably right as design was often an add-on to make things sell better. Today the issue is no longer about using design to sell more products, but about the legitimacy of those products which already exist. Designers, above all, need to question this legitimacy and in doing so may have to make one of the most positive contributions possible – that is, to refuse to take on the commission because an object already exists and functions perfectly well. To re-design it would be a corrupt act with serious consequences: people and the environment would be impoverished.

In order to determine whether a product or commission is legitimate I have set myself some strict parameters. Firstly, I make nothing that may have disastrous consequences for humanity – so despite the financial implications I will not work for companies selling arms, hard alcohol, tobacco or where their funding is questionable. This can become quite complicated so we now insist on a clause in all our contracts which means clients have to divulge their finance sources.

I insist that the product to be designed must either be new, or provide an improved service otherwise one might as well use objects that already exist. It must also have a purity of design and use and be constructed with the minimum of materials. I always cite the example of the client who asked for a boat but found himself very satisfied with the designer's advice recommending that he try swimming instead. This forces him to rediscover old pleasures. The reality is that objects exist in our sub-consciousness outside their specific purpose. So for me it is essential that the designer considers the politics, social, sexual and economic environment and avoids those objects which may represent aggression, violence or fascism.

Objects should never be a means of representing wealth – or be a way of humiliating one's neighbour. Today

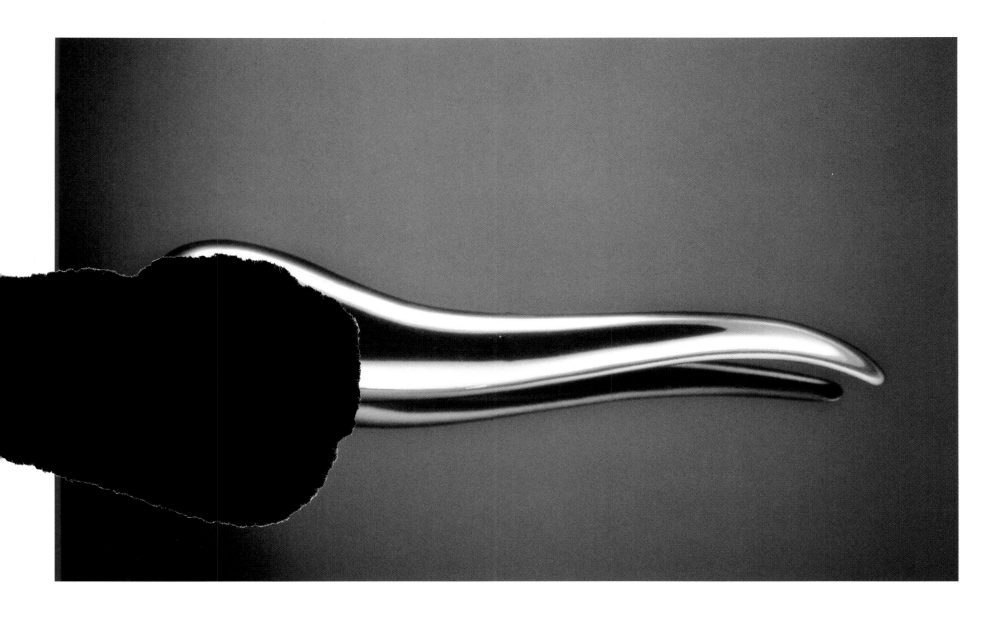

80% of objects are useless so it is essential not to create more elitist products. Good quality should benefit everyone – not just the rich. I believe that you should think about the ethos of businesses, not just the craftsmanship of their products.

As artistic director of Thomson's for four years, my principal task was to return the company to its core values – long since forgotten – namely to provide the best possible service for their customers. It was essential for me to play a type of friendly enemy from within; to encourage them to use their know-how – the financial means, the research, the distribution – to go back to basics. My first act was to change their name from Thomson Consumer Electronics (who wants to be an "electronic consumer"?) to Thomson Multimedia because there's no point in making beautiful television sets if they are perceived as rubbish! I then went on to insist that the anonymity of the word "consumer" was replaced with "my friend," "my wife," "my daughter," "my mother" or "myself". You get a totally different perspective if the phrase is changed from "this is shit but it doesn't matter, the consumers will be satisfied with it" to: "this is shit but it doesn't matter, my daughter will be satisfied with it". I also came up with the slogan "Thomson: from technology to love". The point being that technology is a purely a means to an end – and its purpose is to benefit humanity.

Coming back to the role of the designer, the important thing is not that an object is beautiful but that fundamentally it is "good" for the person who is going to live with it. A product should not be hidden behind logos, nor should it be showy. It must be allowed to brighten up a person's life, to allow them to be themselves (not the extension of a designer) and to be happy with themselves. People are not actors and it is essential that we re-invent ourselves before we disappear under a sea of trademarks and mediocrity.

A good product is one that lasts. When it has lasted ten, twenty, thirty years, at the point where it no longer matters, it may be recycled. But to recycle useless objects every year is a waste of material and of energy. I am

Apriti

Door Handle

Design
Philippe Starck

Client
Ros Kleis
1991

Sesamo

Door Handle

Design
Philippe Starck

Client
Ros Kleis
1991

StarkNaked

combination Dress, Skirt and Tights

Design
Philippe Starck

Client/manufacturer
Wolford
1997

not against recycling, I am against the idea of making it a universal panacea. Recycling is a false solution, a false problem – an ecological cream tart – in the way that it exists today. It is like electric energy for cars, which replaces the exhaust pipe with nuclear power stations.

One of the rare victories in my career was to have elevated the status of mass-produced products – to make good design accessible to all. Take the humble toothbrush: one day it was relegated to the bottom of a drawer and the next it made a great Christmas present. Price is also a key factor. For a decade I successfully reduced the price of my products by almost half every year or two years. One of my earliest projects – the Café Costes chair – sold at 4,000 francs when it was launched. Now it costs no more than 300 francs. Making good design accessible, however, cannot be achieved without a major distribution network.

Good Goods – a collaboration with Carrefour and La Redoute – has been a momentous project and one that is dear to my heart. It has taken more than two years to launch and although I don't regret it, I wouldn't repeat it. My aim with Good Goods was to provide a range of simple, honest products targeted at "modern rebels" – "non-consumers" who are tired of being told by the press or advertising what they should buy. These people represent a new unspoken, political force – the "moral market". They will receive the catalogue with its introduction from me telling them something quite revolutionary in the world of business – that "I have tried to find, collect, correct or create (where necessary) objects which are honest, responsible and respectful to people. Not necessarily beautiful objects, but good objects". Good Goods is one of the biggest operations in the history of design. In effect it creates a chain of 'convenience stores'' open 24 hours a day. With 30,000 "outlets'' (people who receive the catalogue) in Asia of which 8,000 are in Japan, and I don't know how many in the United States, this chain provides everything you would find in a shop – yoghurts, razors, pants, pencils. It is one of the biggest mail order operations in the world. That benefits everybody and is a definite slap in the face to elitist design.

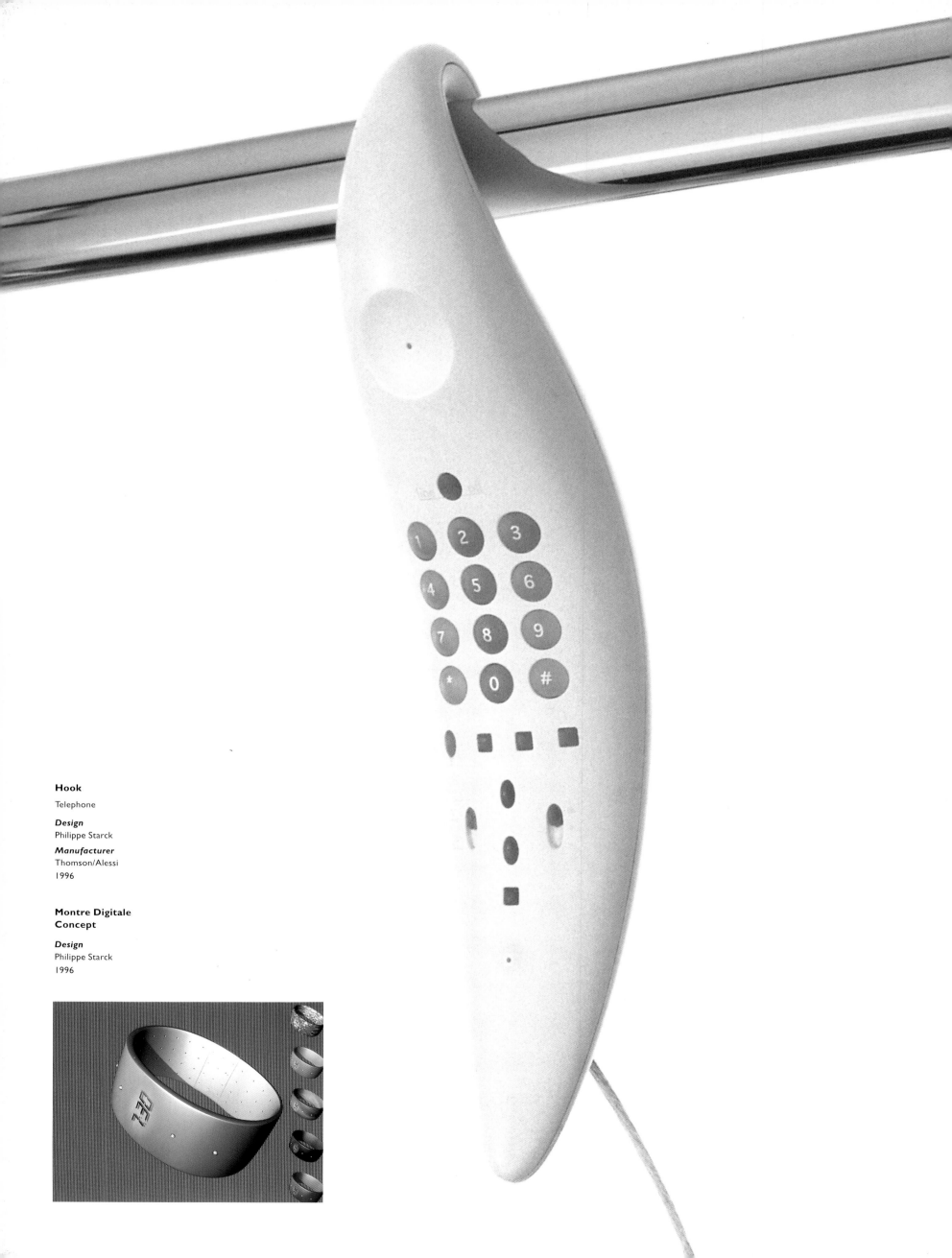

Hook

Telephone

Design
Philippe Starck

Manufacturer
Thomson/Alessi
1996

**Montre Digitale
Concept**

Design
Philippe Starck
1996

M5107
Remote Control Unit

Design
Philippe Starck
Manufacturer
Saba
1994

Jim Nature
Portable TV

Design
Philippe Starck
Client
Saba
1994

Lux Lux
TV

Concept
Philippe Starck
Design
Mike Davison
Manufacturer
Telefunken
1996

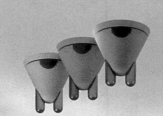

Vercingetorige
Table Alarm Clock

Design
Julian Brown

Client/manufacturer
Rexite Spa
1993

My first project for Rexite and a wonderful moment of discovery, something that had been crying to come out. On the one hand the ruthless search for functional clarity and quintessential simplicity and on the other, the need for the product to speak straight to the heart. The idea of character had never been foremost in my mind (nor is it ever today) but when you see a page of sketches some wink and others do not. 'Vercingetorige' became the perfect vehicle to expand the myth and culture of the product, inherent within its 'odd' helmet like form and expressed itself in the rich and diverse mix of raw as well as sophisticated plastics and optical qualities.

studiobrown

StudioBrown
Julian Brown

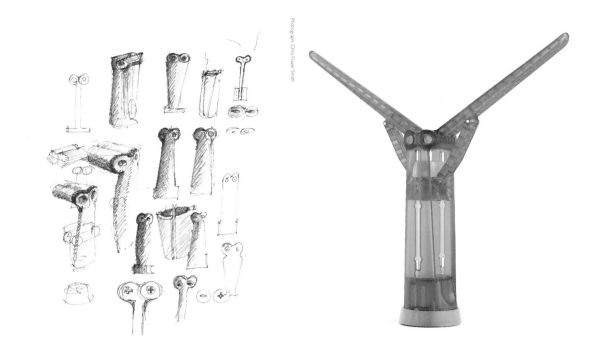

Photograph: Chris Fraser Smith

Attila
Free-Standing Beverage
Can Compactor
Design
Julian Brown
Manufacturer
Rexite Spa
1996

The idea to tackle a 'recycling' product came from Rino Pirovano, commercial director of Rexite, the solution came from a tough and technically demanding analysis of the task of crushing cans. The secret lay in the 'invitation' to recycle by making the process 'fun' and the solution led quickly to a free-standing product. The rest was a labour of love and refinement, with the character leads coming from the product's geometry and a belief that it would all be possible in plastic. None of this could have happened without Rexite's technical director Rino Boscets who ignored advice from Germany's leading injection moulding company that it was 'impossible' and did it his way. To date, not one product has been returned broken.

I came to design completely by chance. Having spent a great year in Dusseldorf after school I entered university to study engineering. Six months into the course and totally despondent I was attracted to a German publication, "Tisch 80", in a vain attempt to test my language skills. It turned out to be a report on a design competition by Rosenthal and was filled with wonderful "inventions" as I understood them at the time, created not by oddballs in garden sheds as the prevailing "Tomorrow's World" culture would have us believe but by "industrial designers". I had never heard that combination of words before. Within a week I had talked my way on to the course of my choice without a single drawing and began to study with a vigour and passion I had only previously experienced building customised motorcycles as a teenage obsession. Something had clicked.

At college Bellini was my idol and his "Karasutra" entry to the "Italy, the New Domestic Landscape" exhibition held at the Museum of Modern Art was electrifying: such poetry and above all, such controversy in the face of contemporary automotive thinking. But this was an architect, not a "product designer" in the specialist sense at the time in the UK. Later at the Royal College of Art I was able to test this growing belief in a more European and versatile design model and concluded my work with a "prophetic" set of studies on electronic products, tableware and furniture. Prophetic, because these remain three of my major areas of involvement today. I also came to appreciate the infinite wealth in the study of simple archetypal items such as a spoon or a coffee cup and combined this with a passion for materials and an ongoing quest to rationalise their use within a functional framework. It was just a question of time before it would all fall into place.

My first true success came during my time with the Porsche Design Studio in Austria with the Studio glasses, a frame which incorporated a minute, mechanically suspended and synchronised leather nose saddle designed specifically for comfort and fit. On presentation of the prototype the client drew the analogy of "slipping your arm into a beautifully tailored jacket". That was good enough for me.

Pump and Go

Transportable Pump Flask

Design
Julian Brown

Client/manufacturer
alfi-Zitzmann
1999

Pump and Go is the first fully
'European' designed pump
flask and establishes a new
and simple language.
Previously all pump flasks
solve the problem of the
protruding spout with various
globular and overstyled
'integrated' forms, resulting in
'elephant man-like' ugliness.
Pump and Go recognises
itself as a vessel, a barrel of
liquid, all that is needed is a
spout. Traditionally, beer taps
are conical pegs, hammered
into an opening perpendicular
to the cylindrical body, just
so, Pump and Go. Lifting the
spout or 'nose' makes it pert
and cheeky, the rest follows
to complete the character
and deliver a new level of
functionality.

La-Ola

Insulated Table Top Jug
Design
Julian Brown

Client/manufacturer
alfi-Zitzmann
1997

The wave is by no means a
new idea, but adapted to
solve the perennial
connection of 'spout', handle'
and 'crown' at the top of an
insulated jug, it can have some
integrity and charm. Formally
though, the cultural soul of La
Ola lies deeper in the past,
within the spirit of the
essential and utilitarian
French enamelled coffee pot.
On its own, the slightly
conical body is a 'non design'
shape (which makes it all the
more interesting to me) but
truncated by the three-
dimensional wave and high
handle, it takes on a
completely modern tableware
identity. Equal credit for the
enormous success of La Ola
goes to George Duemmig-
Zitzmann for forcing a 'low
cost' priority on the design
and in particular, the foot. This
is classic hard core industrial
design delivering a lot, for
very little, to many.

Isis

Stapler

Design
Julian Brown

Manufacturer
Rexite Spa
1999

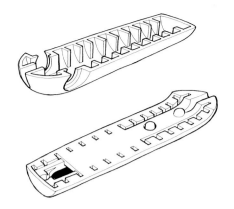

Hannibal has longed for a sister for too long and finally Isis will keep him company. Elephants and crocodiles may be the final manifestation but this project grew from the awareness that no-one was making high quality 'plastic' desk tools. Traditionally, the stapler is either a 'zero value' office commodity or a highly priced solid metal executive accessory, our aim was to create a high quality 'plastic' middleground. The simple charm of the Rexite products belie the complexity of their mechanisms and the level of investment but will be here for as long as staples are stapled and tape is taped. They are designed as 'standards'.

Hannibal

Tape Dispenser

Design
Julian Brown

Manufacturer
Rexite Spa
1998

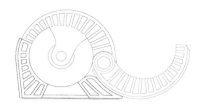
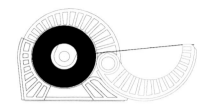

Of all my work for Rexite, Hannibal speaks with the clearest voice, he may well be technical, a tour de force of visual and engineering plastic qualities, but he simply has magic. This is a great feeling and some vindication of the idea that manufactured objects really can have value beyond the bottom line. Once again though, this charm is not applied but results from an almost obsessive search for functional performance and geometric integrity together with a kind eye looking for the character to emerge. This is a strange territory, lying somewhere between Bauhaus and Disney.

Twelve years on I know a little more. I have run my own studio for nine years within a very competitive business. To rise above the homogeneity of "service design" offerings you have to be your own man and positively promote individual qualities. I now enjoy great success with my work but know that without the client there would be nothing: no thread, no connection, no spirit; they are the amplifier through which I speak. The trick is to find the right words but never lose your voice.

I love and hate the first moments of a project, that forced sense of humility, ignorance and naivety that allow the crucial insight into a product. There is a sense of insecurity and a scrabbling to find a foothold, something small but undiscovered, something dormant but a key. I create an imaginary framework for evaluating ideas full of words or "attitudes" that orientate decisions and eventually converge the process. Everything has a floating value or weight in the final balance, comfort, line, colour, danger, material, light, cost, charm, wit, process, you name it. Eventually the haze distils and you are left with a cohesive story, a composition with a clear and distinct concept, an idea, one that fits. Then comes the fun bit. I confess to being something of a geometry or shape freak, but there is no shape without purpose and there is no life without soul. I do not create soul or spirit, I find it. If you take the right road you will eventually get to where you want to go.

A lovely example is the Hannibal tape dispenser for Rexite of Milan. The core geometry came from a study of the tape roll, the action of pulling and cutting and the need to prevent slipping. Over time I have evolved a quintessential "monoform" language of shape for Rexite products each which requires the discovery of a simple, almost primary, volume. In this case all I needed was a single shape to encapsulate all the points – and 'abracadabra! The trick was finding the broken circle, the transformation between closed and open, the accidental genius of the tape re-tensioning itself and of course the elephant. What a fantastic moment! After this is an equally enjoyable and absolutely critical part, not the technical drawing of yesterday, but the final

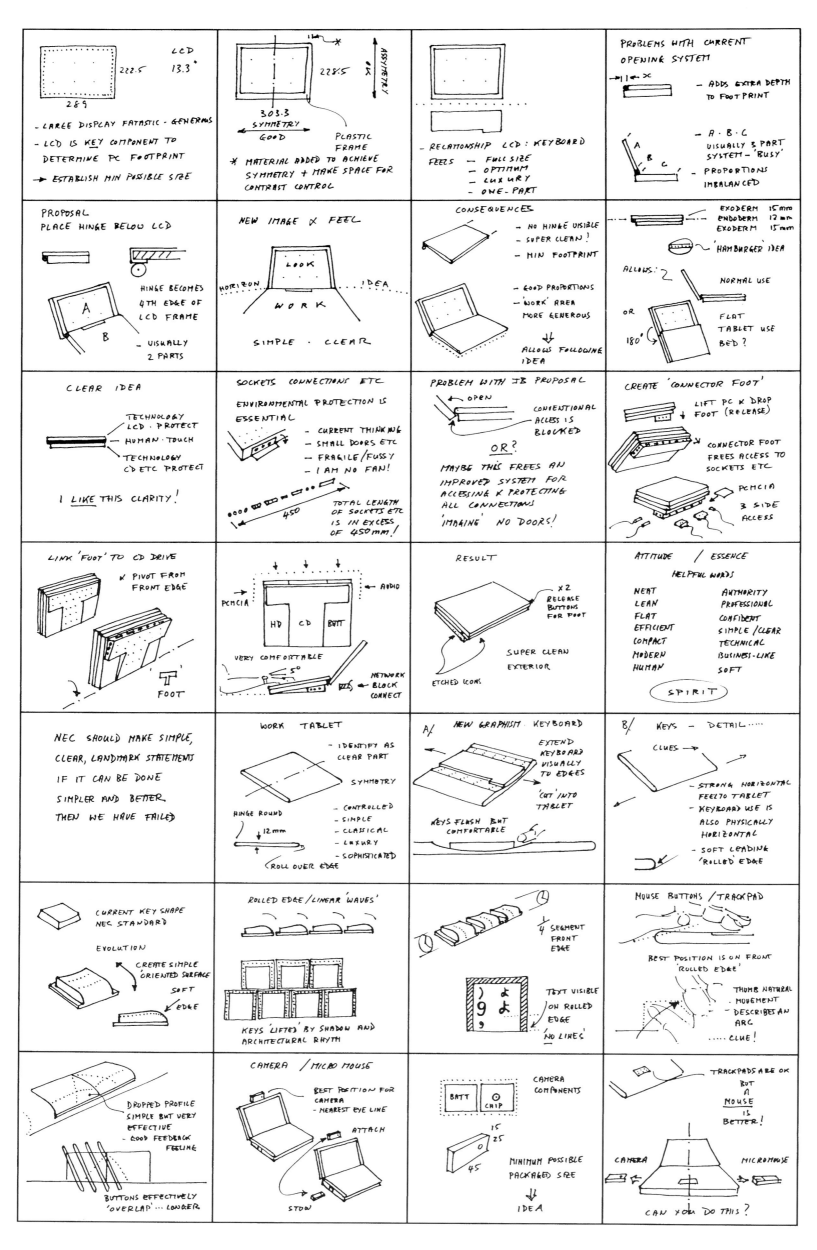

LCD 13.3"
222.5 / 289
- LARGE DISPLAY FANTASTIC - GENEROUS
- LCD IS KEY COMPONENT TO DETERMINE PC FOOTPRINT
→ ESTABLISH MIN POSSIBLE SIZE

228.5
303.3 SYMMETRY GOOD
PLASTIC FRAME — ASYMMETRY
* MATERIAL ADDED TO ACHIEVE SYMMETRY + MAKE SPACE FOR CONTRAST CONTROL

- RELATIONSHIP LCD : KEYBOARD FEELS
  — FULL SIZE
  — OPTIMUM
  — LUXURY
  — ONE-PART

PROBLEMS WITH CURRENT OPENING SYSTEM
- ADDS EXTRA DEPTH TO FOOTPRINT
A·B·C
- A·B·C USUALLY 3 PART SYSTEM - 'BUSY'
- PROPORTIONS IMBALANCED

PROPOSAL
PLACE HINGE BELOW LCD
HINGE BECOMES 4TH EDGE OF LCD FRAME
A / B
- VISUALLY 2 PARTS

NEW IMAGE & FEEL
HORIZON ... IDEA
LOOK / WORK
SIMPLE · CLEAR

CONSEQUENCES
- NO HINGE VISIBLE
- SUPER CLEAN!
- MIN FOOTPRINT
- GOOD PROPORTIONS
- 'WORK' AREA MORE GENEROUS
↓ ALLOWS FOLLOWING IDEA

EXODERM 15mm / ENDODERM 12mm / EXODERM 15mm
'HAMBURGER IDEA'
ALLOWS:
NORMAL USE
OR 180°
FLAT TABLET USE BED?

CLEAR IDEA
TECHNOLOGY LCD · PROTECT
HUMAN · TOUCH
TECHNOLOGY CD ETC PROTECT
I LIKE THIS CLARITY!

SOCKETS CONNECTIONS ETC
ENVIRONMENTAL PROTECTION IS ESSENTIAL
- CURRENT THINKING
- SMALL DOORS ETC
- FRAGILE/FUSSY
- I AM NO FAN!
450
TOTAL LENGTH OF SOCKETS ETC IS IN EXCESS OF 450mm!

PROBLEM WITH JB PROPOSAL
OPEN
CONVENTIONAL ACCESS IS BLOCKED
OR?
MAYBE THIS FREES AN IMPROVED SYSTEM FOR ACCESSING & PROTECTING ALL CONNECTIONS 'IMAGINE' NO DOORS!

CREATE 'CONNECTOR FOOT'
LIFT PC & DROP FOOT (RELEASE)
CONNECTOR FOOT FREES ACCESS TO SOCKETS ETC
PCMCIA 3 SIDE ACCESS

LINK 'FOOT' TO CD DRIVE
& PIVOT FROM FRONT EDGE
FOOT

PCMCIA — AUDIO
HD CD BATT
VERY COMFORTABLE
5°
NETWORK BLOCK CONNECT

RESULT
x2 RELEASE BUTTONS FOR FOOT
SUPER CLEAN EXTERIOR
ETCHED ICONS

ATTITUDE / ESSENCE
HELPFUL WORDS
NEAT / LEAN / FLAT / EFFICIENT / COMPACT / MODERN / HUMAN
AUTHORITY / PROFESSIONAL / CONFIDENT / SIMPLE / CLEAR / TECHNICAL / BUSINESS-LIKE / SOFT
(SPIRIT)

NEC SHOULD MAKE SIMPLE, CLEAR, LANDMARK STATEMENT IF IT CAN BE DONE SIMPLER AND BETTER THEN WE HAVE FAILED

WORK TABLET
- IDENTIFY AS CLEAR PART
- SYMMETRY
- CONTROLLED
- SIMPLE
- CLASSICAL
- LUXURY
- SOPHISTICATED
HINGE ROUND 12mm
'ROLL OVER EDGE'

A/ NEW GRAPHISM KEYBOARD
EXTEND KEYBOARD VISUALLY TO EDGES
'CUT INTO TABLET'
KEYS FLUSH BUT COMFORTABLE

B/ KEYS - DETAIL .....
CLUES →
- STRONG HORIZONTAL FEEL TO TABLET
- KEYBOARD USE IS ALSO PHYSICALLY HORIZONTAL
- SOFT LEADING 'ROLLED EDGE'

CURRENT KEY SHAPE NEC STANDARD
EVOLUTION
CREATE SIMPLE ORIENTED SURFACE
SOFT EDGE

ROLLED EDGE/LINEAR 'WAVES'
KEYS 'LIFTED' BY SHADOW AND ARCHITECTURAL RHYTHM

4 SEGMENT FRONT EDGE
TEXT VISIBLE ON ROLLED EDGE 'NO LINES'

MOUSE BUTTONS / TRACKPAD
BEST POSITION IS ON FRONT 'ROLLED EDGE'
THUMB NATURAL MOVEMENT - DESCRIBES AN ARC ..... CLUE!

DROPPED PROFILE SIMPLE BUT VERY EFFECTIVE
- GOOD FEEDBACK FEELING
BUTTONS EFFECTIVELY 'OVERLAP' ... LONGER

CAMERA / MICRO MOUSE
BEST POSITION FOR CAMERA - NEAREST EYE LINE
ATTACH
STOW

CAMERA COMPONENTS
BATT / CHIP
15 / 25 / 45
MINIMUM POSSIBLE PACKAGED SIZE
↓ IDEA

TRACKPADS ARE OK BUT A MOUSE IS BETTER!
CAMERA / MICROMOUSE
CAN YOU DO THIS?

La Vie

Laptop computer

Design
Julian Brown

Manufacturer
NEC Design
1997

The sequence of sketches is a direct copy of a presentation made to NEC Design at the concept stage. I particularly like it because it is raw and honest and demonstrates the power of rationale over showmanship. In fact the whole project hung on this communication.

I had converged on a single, powerful and clear concept, not just another detail 'work-over' but a careful re-assessment of a number of standard, 'laptop' issues. Had the response been negative, the project would have died. I had to wait two long days to hear – what I love about working with the Japanese is that they never rush decisions and are eminently respectful of your every thought. The reply came, "these are big ideas" and the project sped ahead.

composition of the product. The individual ingredients have been defined but their contribution needs careful direction, the marriage of physical and visual material qualities together with manufacturing processes and above all the manipulation of character. You can push it, pull it, exaggerate it, kill it even, but the fun is finding that special territory between smile and joke, charm and ridicule, even Disney and Bauhaus. But that is for Rexite.

In total contrast, my work for NEC uses an identical mind but the spirit is found elsewhere. With the Laptop project my aim was to redefine a set of design values, not just shapes, which would help re-position NEC as a leading and authoritative force in PC design. Size (or lack of it) is an unassailable quality in the perception of neatness and practicality in portable computers. Add a blown surface over a flat component and you get fat, you are carrying "air". Be the company with the slimmest, tightest and highest specification packages and you will have authority. Do it with a level of refinement, a new graphical sophistication and a quality of detail that melts into the fingers when touched and you have a new perception of servile technology. This is tough country, with little room for manoeuvre, uninhabited by the makeover stylists, yet there is abundant fruit. The simple moving of the opening hinge below the visual horizon creates a new calm and easy binary relationship between the touch and look-at parts. This in turn forces a big idea, as the Japanese call it, in the discovery of a new, single click, dropdown monobloc connector foot. Gone are the itsy bitsy doors and in their place a solution which inclines the product comfortably, opens ventilation space, eliminating the need for a power-hungry fan and finally enables you to squeeze in a remote micro mouse and plug-on internet video camera. Now we can talk about the shape, the feel, the sophistication...

Rotor 2000
Outdoor Public Telephone

Client
I.P.M. Naples
1998

studio sowden

Studio Sowden Design Associates
George J. Sowden

Jack
Project for F.M. Radio

Client
Alessi
1997

Studio Sowden consists of eight people in 300 square metres of industrial space, formerly the warehouse of a glassware supplier to pharmaceutical companies. From a rational point of view we have much more space than we need, but a lot of it is used to keep models, prototypes or drawings so the interior design is really an accumulation of studio work and research. Although there is a well-defined computer space the rest is general areas for meetings and social activities.

Studio Sowden has always researched and paid particular attention to the nature of the object, the language of design, the way products are identified. I try to avoid the inevitable paranoia created by uncertainty and a lack of communication. I like to think that above all we make an effort to be poetic.

We now work almost exclusively on the design and engineering of electronic or electro-technical products for industrial production.

Since 1994, Studio Sowden has comprised four partners: George J. Sowden, Hiroshi Ono, Davy Kho and Franco Mele. However, the history of the office covers a period of the last 25 or so years and is made up of many different strata: my own radical years of 70s design research, parallel with early work for Olivetti and the design of their first electro-mechanical and later electronic products. Followed, in the 80s, by the Memphis years, together with my increasing curiosity about the evolving identity of electronic consumer products. The studio laid down layers of experience with various kinds of industrially manufactured products as well as artisan products such as textiles, glass and ceramics.

I studied architecture at Gloucester College of Art in the 60s. I came to Milan looking for work as an architect and went to see Sottsass. He offered me a job and sent me to Olivetti where I became a designer working with all those wonderful engineers who had made Olivetti into an internationally recognised company. I remember my first experience at Olivetti: walking into a huge drawing office and seeing maybe 50 to 100 drawing boards;

Dauphine

Desktop Calculator

Client
Alessi
1997

Alphonse

Electronic Timer

Client
Alessi
1997

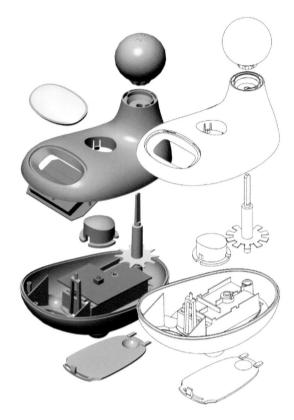

on each one a different drawing. It was a place which controlled information in a way which I later defined as the manual management of information. It was there that I learnt the complexity involved in handling industrial processes and where design fits into all that. But there, in the 70s and 80s, I learnt the old 2-D system involving hundreds of people, drawing boards, sheets of paper passed from hand to hand, corrections, infinite revisions of part-codes and the constant effort to avoid mistakes. But it was that experience which helped me to discover the creative possibilities and the quality advantages made available to us as the studio moved into electronic management of information at the beginning of the 90s. We learnt how to model and engineer electronically, moving enormous amounts of 3-D information using just a few people.

We took part in a revolution in industrial design which of course was a consequence of a de-industrial revolution which was happening in industrial organisations. And, as we moved through the 90s, the whole world restructured its industrial attitude: smaller companies taking the lead over mastodontic multinationals. Products started appearing in continuous, almost organic, production cycles and not as the result at the end of a long linear process, as had been until very recently.

Studio Sowden recognised this change early on and we are now capable of handling complex industrial processes using advanced electronic systems. At the same time everyone in the office is constantly brainstorming. We work on bits of paper, sketches and soft models before working up computer information. We have become very good at selecting and rejecting quickly... I like to think our process is more organic than linear. Individual talent, quietness and being alone and thinking about things is of the utmost importance. But in the end, what comes out of the office is the result of group working. There is a constant synthesis in which the client plays a big part.

Nene

Short Message Recorder
Key Ring

Client
Milan Pacific, USA
1998

T.U.O.

Indoor Public Telephone

Client
Telecom Italia
1997

T.U.O. is part of Telecom's
strategy to install more public
telephone services in bars,
shops, hospitals, schools etc.
This product can be desk or
wall-mounted and is moulded
in ABS plastic.

The way the office works would be impossible without the electronic management – the speed at which we process information creates energy around the project, conveys the idea of pleasure in creating and makes space to involve other people in the development. It is important to be as dynamic as possible and to never stop pushing until the product is very well defined. I believe that this is evident in the finished product.

The nature of the studio's work is determined by the fact that we design and engineer simultaneously; to divide them would be artificial. The way that things are assembled is so important, as it is in fashion or music. The engineering in products is like the quality of the cut in clothes or the sensitivity of the touch in music. Engineering is the execution.

Manufacturing needs to be done carefully. Modern aesthetics, like modern lifestyles, are very fragile. I do not mean this in a weak sense, I mean they are fast, they disregard monumentality, they depend on diversity. But, they rely on quality as we build a collage of unrelated objects that become the world in which we live. Quality, in the end, is the skill and ability to manage all the information to come up with the finished product.

Society lives fast. We consume simultaneously as we turn the page in the magazine and glance across the street, our attention caught as the taxi turns the corner in a hurry, as the lights are changing. All that surrounds us is artificial, each time different, exceptional, sometimes surprising, but always communicative. (There is always a sentiment.) It is the quality of communication that has become the driving force of the world, a driving force that pushes in at all levels, organisational and cultural, changing our behavioural patterns. I believe it is unrealistic to want to put order into our environment. It is the complexity and the instability of the present that gives it its strength, and the constantly changing undergrowth through the transfusion of ideas that gives it its vitality. Do we ever see the same thing twice?

Rotor 2000

Outdoor Public Telephone

Client
I.P.M. Naples
1998

A. Product modular concept

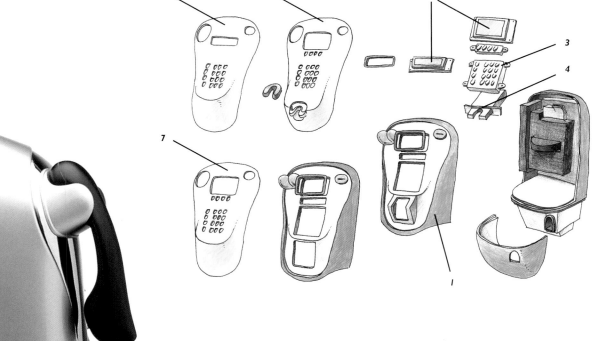

B. Mathematical engineering – computer models

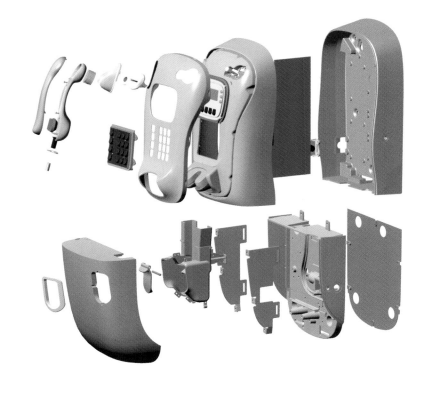

C. Keypad module

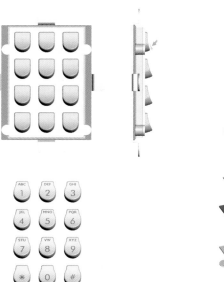

Modelling

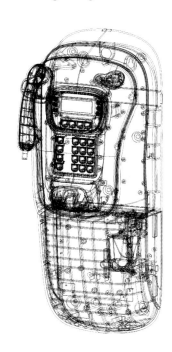

Engineering

Presentation

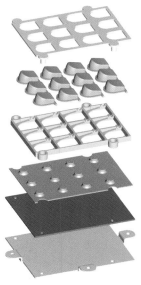

Rotor 2000

Outdoor Public Telephone

Client
I.P.M. Naples
1998

A. Product modular concept

One of the principal specifications of this new public pay phone was the need to be able to configure it to suit different functions. This was achieved by designing a technical panel-door (1) that could accept the mounting of various modules (2-3-4). The aesthetic panels (5-6-7) cover those mounting points not being used in a particular configuration.

B. Mathematical engineering – computer models

Studio Sowden considers engineering and design to be an integrated process that would be artificial to separate. The nature of the studio's work is determined by the fact that we design and engineer at the same time. The way that things are assembled is so important, as in fashion or music. The engineering in products is like the quality of the cut in clothes or the sensitivity of the touch in music. Engineering is the execution.

C. Keypad module

Each internal module was designed and engineered specifically for the product. In the case of the keyboard pad, where a rotation key provides better ergonomics and visibility, the front and middle panels are aluminium die-cast pieces with a steel backing to ensure that the keyboard is resistant. The display module (2) was conceived in a similar way. Different display sizes and configurations can be accommodated.

D. Computer engineering – computer protoype

One of the advantages of the electronic management of information is the possibility to create virtual prototypes where fitting and tolerances can be decided upon and checked before moving into the workshop to build real prototypes. In this case the images show the assembly of the three interface modules of the Rotor 2000 (the display unit, the keyboard unit and the card-reader unit).

E. Product family development

The modular concept of the phone allows it to be configured in different ways starting from a combined 'coins and card' unit, followed by a version of 'coins only', 'cards only', 'cards and fax', and 'ISDN electronics' up to an all-electronic phone which uses touch-screen technology to allow internet access and information services. All the major external pieces are die-cast aluminium with the exception of the front aesthetic panel which is pressed steel, and the handset which is moulded ABS plastic.

D. Computer engineering – computer prototypes

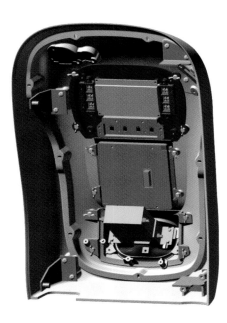

E. Product family development – computer images

top row left to right:
– cards only
– ISDN
– ISDN with receipt printer
bottom row left to right:
– coins and cards
– coins only
– cards and fax
– touch access web phone

Coin Phone Final Product

159

GCS DECT

Phone

Client
GCS
1997

The DECT phone is a design that combines curvaceous forms with technical expression. It offers the benefit of digital technologies at home or in the office. The intent behind the appearance is to focus on the home environment but still have qualities which express technology in a calm and controlled way. The colour scheme is light metallic, which relates to the home and still maintains a technical association.

tangerine

tangerine
Martin Darbyshire

Concept Fax Machine
Concept Home
Facsimile

Design
tangerine
1990

Market precedence can be challenged. Insight into the needs of the home-user led us to change the internal format of existing fax machines to create this thought provoking 'niche' product. By analysing format you can radically change the look of a product. The fax occupies a minimum space whilst providing a decorative function to compliment the domestic interior. It allows any format of printed material to be faxed (be it a book, photograph or hand-written greeting) and is operated in conjunction with a standard telephone.

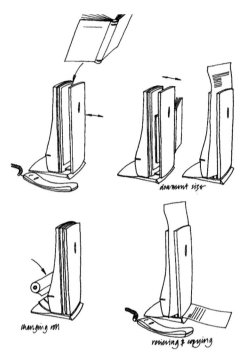

The thing that drove me to design was coming from a family of engineers. In my home, simple, pragmatic things were dominant forces in decision-making. The essential soft qualitative values of objects rarely took precedence.

At school what motivated me the most was a blend of technical drawing and art, both of which were well resourced. There were two teachers who were particularly influential in my development. I was the only 'A' level art student who went on to further education in the arts. As such a rarity, I was hauled into the Headmaster's office to learn of my place at the then Central School of Art and Design. Since graduating in 1983 I have worked purely in consultancy in the UK and USA. Deep down the aspects of design which really appeal to me, but are by far the most difficult to address, are locating and defining the aesthetic qualities of objects that make them right. To become successful you need to be able to quantify the sensual and emotional characteristics of objects so that you can help explain their quantities. One of the biggest problems in design is not creating the object itself but selling it on and convincing people it is the right object to buy. There are many designers who are producing work that we would say "look as though they've been designed". What drives me is a passion to really delve into the emotional and aesthetic qualities of these objects and to try and explore them. This was something that I found difficult to do at college since, at that time, industrial design was still very heavily about rationalising things, about taking machinery and making it safe or making it look comprehensible; taking industrial machinery, painting it grey and putting little yellow disks on the hinges. The interest for me is taking it way beyond that. It's not about raw functionality, it's about the really complex emotional qualities that make something right for people, or make it totally wrong. Part of that is making it comfortable, familiar but still something you want to really have and keep.

Apple Computer

Design
tangerine

Client
Apple
1990

The brief, an exploration of portable computers in different user scenarios, led to the expression of three themes in physical concept models. These concepts provided both a view of future products, allowing Apple to reposition and evaluate their company goals and provided an insight into aspects of use which are seldom uncovered unless a concept is made real. 'Sketchpad' (shown here) is designed for 'use on the move', is very portable and has the abilities of a Newton. 'Workspace' (not shown) allows users to move easily between desk and home. 'Folio' (not shown) provides a flexible approach with the added benefit of use on the move with a pen not a keyboard, a cordless keyboard, detached mouse and calculator.

I was one of two partners that formed tangerine in 1989. From the start we set our ambitions high and emphasised the creative upstream aspects of planning, research and design. For some considerable time we have flowed against a tide of competitors who have given priority to downstream development, such as concurrent engineering and rapid prototyping. Our approach has since proven to be a wise investment.

tangerine is about getting to the heart of a product within the context of a business strategy. It's about making products *be* designed, not just *look* like they have been designed. The culture of tangerine's studio is fun and dynamic but also extremely hard work. It's a blend of things. As a team we realise both design strategy and policy strategy together. We listen and learn from each other. Whilst there is no one big ego motivating one direction, there is no shortage of talent and ambition – or egos!

Since forming 10 years ago, the focus of tangerine has never changed, but the scope and potential for product design has. Where the traditional role of product design has been reactive, designing a metal/plastic box around a circuit board, it is now part of the integral planning of the communication strategy of a company.

Generally it is unlikely that any designer can fundamentally affect the key technology components of a project. So a major concern of product design must be understanding how any one product expresses its heritage and brand values, and at the same time makes it individual and connect to people. Products must connect in the right way with the people who sell, buy and use them.

On the one hand product design is frequently about wrapping plastic shapes around bits of hardware. But to do that well designers and manufacturers must understand customers' desires and aspirations, and embody them in the core values of a product. This can't be done unless you have established a close association with the client and developed planning, research and design strategies together. tangerine has worked with LG Electronics for over eight years and we are now in a position to affect whole sets of products through this approach.

Blink

Concept Digital Camera &
Electronic Photo Album

Design
tangerine
1993

Designed as part of Products
for the New Era, a Japanese
competition, the brief was to
create future thinking designs
for comfortable styles of
living – in particular for
an ageing population. As a
competition piece, tangerine
was able to focus on user-
centred problems without
too much consideration of
cost parameters. As a result,
they created a digital camera
and picture viewer which is
simple to use and allows even
the most inexperienced
photographer to take
successful pictures. Once
taken, pictures are stored
digitally on a removable
cartridge which has a similar
form to that of a 35mm film
cannister to give familiarity to
the older user. These
concepts are real products
for the future which made
use of the potential of digital
storage and LCD imaging as
well as giving the camera
character and value by losing
the black plastic, throwaway
quality of many of the
cameras at the time.

Brian Drumm

Flatliner Comb

Design
tangerine
1995

The Flatliner comb is a haircutting tool used in professional hair salons in the UK, USA and Japan for hairstyling that requires a straight edge. Initially, the comb was presented as a series of colour renderings and foam models. The model itself was extremely accurate and showed the finer details and form of the product. The comb is unique because of the spirit level that is incorporated into the design enabling hairdressers to use a range of cutting techniques to create styles accurately. The smoothly contoured design allows the stylist to hold the comb comfortably in the palm of the hand or between the thumb and forefinger as well as giving the product a streamlined and stylish appearance. It is finished in a matt, metallic silver, that fits perfectly with the fashion conscious hairdressing salons as well as giving the item an appearance of quality. Flatliner won the IF International Design Award in 1995.

Activ

Walking Frame

Design
tangerine
1998

A drab but functional product, the walking frame has long confirmed the 'medical model' of disability. By contrast, Activ, turns this notion on its head. Designed to take the medical out of mobility, it came about as result of a major research project carried out by the 'Design for Ability' group at Central Saint Martin's College for Art and Design. A survey of 600 adults with physical disabilities was conducted and revealed five distinct consumer groups, opening up the possibility of products being designed with appropriate focus on the psychological needs of the users. This data – which holds significant commercial potential – was tested by tangerine in its redesign of the walking frame. The resulting full-scale model illustrates how such data can impact on the design's understanding and thinking. Activ's materials and appearance are appropriate to the target consumer's needs. The product is height adjustable and folds flat for storage or transportation and an integrated sliding tray can be used to carry meals, drinks or personal items from room to room. Initial market research shows that the design meets the needs of the consumer audience at exactly the right level.

LG Vacuum Cleaner

Design
tangerine
Client
LG Electronics
1998

The brief to tangerine was to research and design a canister-style vacuum cleaner for the European market. Drawing on previous experience in this sector, tangerine created a unique image for the Goldstar brand, enabling LG Electronics to compete more effectively with the likes of Hoover, Electrolux and Rowenta. Typical problems encountered in the research phase related to weight, manoeuvrability, access to tools and user perceptions. From this, four concepts were designed each highlighting solutions to specific problems. The main innovation in this evolutionary design comes from storing the tools in the handle area – making them 'to hand' thus reducing the need for the user to keep returning to the cleaner. One of the tools has a dual function, so two tools cover three separate cleaning functions. Mounting the tools in this way removes the need for the storage door on the body of the cleaner allowing it to have a more continuous, fluid shape and making it smaller and lighter to carry. An added benefit is the location of the on/off switch to the handle. The lower sections of the body are manufactured in soft rubber which acts as a bumper to protect furniture against knocks. An ergonomically-shaped plastic handle incorporated half0way along the hose pipe has been designed as a 'grab handle' aiding manoeuvrability of the cleaner during use.

165

Ultimately where does this approach go? In understanding the core values of a product and what it is that connects the customer to that product, the designer can start to predict what it is that people will want to have in the future and how they will use them. The most far-reaching challenge for design is centred on observing and capturing human behaviour and from this finding new product paradigms. The Sony Walkman is by far the best example of this.

Within tangerine we plan and develop concept designs to stimulate the designers and allow them to develop a freedom of thought and take a strategic approach. These don't always result in an object based on a mechanism; they are holistic responses to human desires and needs. It is difficult for us to justify having people, on a full time basis, from different disciplines. When you are a relatively small team it's very difficult to keep the dynamics of business if you are spread out over many different disciplines and specialist areas. So to date we have collaborated with other groups who are experts in their field. In the future this may change.

No matter how strategic our work becomes, our future still lies in creativity, it is just the process by which the creativity is applied that will be different.

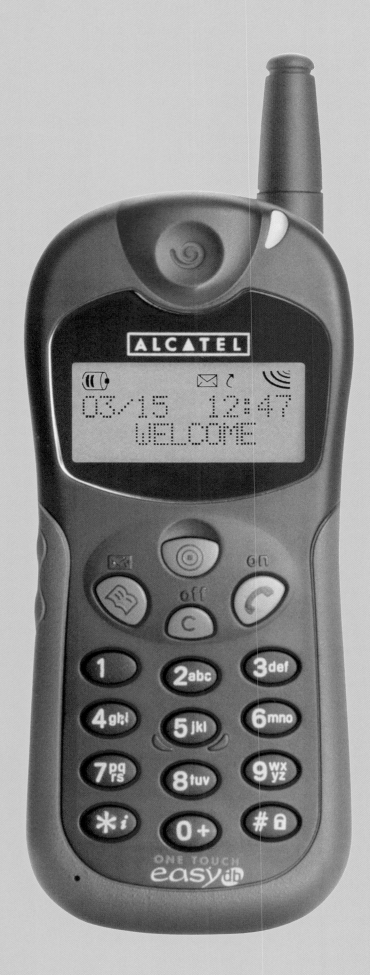

BE1 - One Touch Easy

Dual Band Mobile Telephone

Design
Andy Davey,
Rochelle Smith (TKO),
Vincent Creance,
Anne Bigand (Alcatel),
Paola Pinnavaia (On Design)

Account Handler
Annie Gardener (TKO)

Client/manufacturer
Alcatel Telecom

Design Group
TKO Product Design
1999

tko

TKO

Andy Davey

Laptop
Design Prototype

Design
Andy Davey,
Rochelle Smith (TKO),
Yuichiro Oka,
Keigo Kawasaki
(NEC Design Ltd)

Account Handler
Annie Gardener (TKO)

Client/manufacturer
NEC Design Ltd

Design Group
TKO Product Design
1997

Magic Paintbrush
Children's "Take-Anywhere"
Paintbrush

Design
Andy Davey (TKO),
Paul Horton (Hasbro Europe)

Inventor
Richard Mitzman

Account Handler
Annie Gardener (TKO)

Manufacturer
Lion Brush Ltd

Client
Hasbro Europe

Design Group
TKO Product Design
1995

What does TKO mean? Well, the answer is firmly rooted in the original concept behind the firm's creation, which is effectively to make a "flat pyramid" structure with a memorable brand identity, independent of the individuals involved.

The design scene, particularly in the UK, is fixated by 'surname fame' – Blah and Blah, or Blah Design, or Blah and Co. What this often does, apart from making design companies sound like firms of accountants, is create a company culture where only Blah gets credit for the design output, and a vertical hierarchy develops. The current media obsession with named individual 'creators' – as if the design process is down to a lone creative source – exemplifies this situation. Most commonly, design (especially that of product, packaging and graphics) is a collaborative exercise. So, what does TKO mean, apart from 'democratic'? It is a simple abbreviation of ToKyO – Japan has been a constant source of inspiration and opportunity for TKO since its inception – so it's an acknowledgement of that. If you don't buy that, try Technical Knock-Out instead. Suit yourself.

Although TKO has always been, and I hope always will be, firmly connected with Japanese companies and Japanese culture, it still feels right to be based in central London. The thing about London, like most capitals, is that if you are based in a large city, you should make it in the centre, where the most interesting bits are. I think Clerkenwell is an interesting bit: it has a great tradition of independent trades – watch and clock making, jewellery, printing and newspapers as well as its mediaeval history of the Knights of St John, Saint Bartholemew's Church and Hospital, Charterhouse, Smithfield market and now a creative community.

TKO's present office is a five-storey Georgian house (1805) which has a great ambience, and although it isn't really ideal for communication, it feels right. The combination of restrained Georgian proportions and style and

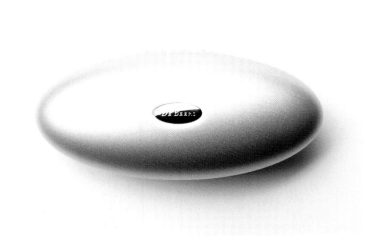

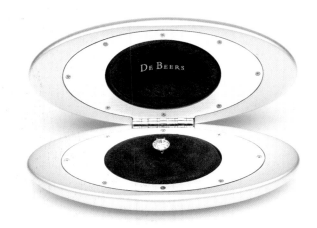

Capsule

Diamond Packaging

Design
Andy Davey, Annie Gardener,
Aaron McKenzie (TKO),
Chris Pring, Jill Dawson
(Bullitt Design)

Account Handler
Annie Gardener (TKO)

Manufacturer
Due DM

Client
De Beers

Design Group
TKO Product Design
1999

168

contemporary design has a certain dynamic. Although the vertical aspect of the building is not always convenient, the building has really positive karma and very good light. There's also a warmth and bustle about the place that makes it very easy to work late, to entertain clients, and still always find a quiet room to just go and chill.

TKO is a compact studio, and we have always tried to maintain a feeling that everyone can do anything and not be too pigeonholed. Choosing to stay small also means you don't have to spend a lot of time chasing work you'd rather not do just because you need the zeros. We have found benefit in creating contacts with specialist groups and freelancers, who can be attached to relevant projects where necessary. In my experience, successful product design has always been based on the collaboration of individuals and teams (both consultancy and in-house), but often the difficult thing is to achieve a sympathetic relationship between team members in terms of approach and objectives. TKO can build a bespoke team for specific projects where the individuals already have a bond.

Our relationship with Japan and Japanese companies has been the cornerstone of TKO's development, and a good deal of the reputation that TKO now enjoys is based on our experiences and projects there. Notions of building relationships with companies and individuals over a long period; of a mutual investment; of personal recommendations; professionalism and trust in individuals – these are qualities I've found operating most strongly in the Japanese business community and which we've tried to build into TKO's way of working.

My passports say that I have visited Japan at least 40 times over the last nine years, and every time some more creative baggage comes back with me. I just love the qualities, the contradictions, and the fundamentals of the

Crystal Mu

LCD Computer
Display System

Design
Andy Davey (TKO),
Yuichiro Oka, Junko Misawa
(NEC Design Ltd)

Account Handler
Annie Gardener (TKO)

Client/manufacturer
NEC Design Ltd
1996

Comet

Low Voltage Lighting System

Design
Andy Davey (TKO),
Hiroshi Nakagawa
(Daiko Electric Co)

Account Handler
Annie Gardener (TKO)

Manufacturer
Daiko Electric Co Ltd

Design Group
TKO Product Design
1992

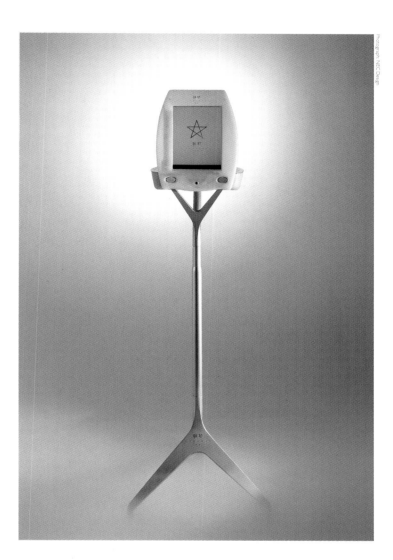

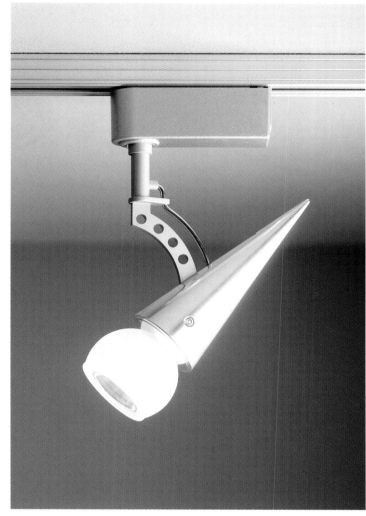

Japanese way of doing things. I have always aspired to, and taken great pride in working with some of the best companies in the world, and during the life of TKO that's exactly what I have wanted to achieve. There is only one problem – I find flying a depressing and synthetic experience that doesn't improve with age or seat width, but well, how tough can it be?

As an industry, design has a huge capacity – there is so much of it going on, some good, much of it bad. But I have always felt that the word "design" isn't rich enough to distinguish normal creative thought processes from truly original thinking. As an everyday word, design has also been duffed-up by the media – often used to mean something wide or unwholesome (like "designer-drugs" – what does that mean?). Despite the fact that there's a lot of "design" about, the rarefied air at the top is still fine and clear. It's easy to see the good designers up there and there aren't too many of them...

In fact, design is no longer a good enough word to describe the nuances and subtleties that have crept into a designer's repertoire of abilities – reactivity to social and technological situations experienced for the first time ever needs a sense of perspective and potential that only the best designers can achieve and others have to aspire to.

Frenzied timescales and cut-throat budgeting can crush the essential elements that go to make an outstanding (rather than okay) product. Product design by its nature cannot be very spontaneous or immediate, but the original idea, and a crucial deftness in handling form, can be. Realising a product that still captures the essence of the original concept is the tricky bit. Design that stays true to an original idea always attracts me – its rightness and refusal to compromise usually shine through – producing, for me, a mixture of delight and jealousy.

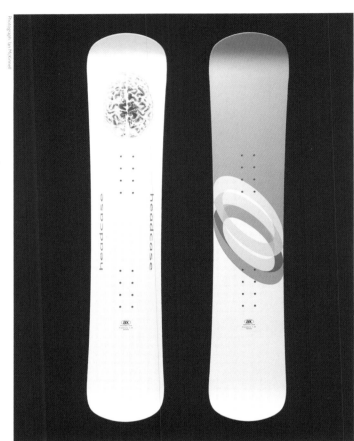

Titan

Washing Machine

Design
Andy Davey, Annie Gardener,
Rochelle Smith (TKO),
Martin Myerscough
(Monotub), Henry Slack
(Cock & Hen)

Account Handler
Annie Gardener

Client
Monotub Industries plc

Design Group
TKO Product Design
1999/2000

Headcase

Prototype Snowboards

Design
Andy Davey,
Rochelle Smith (TKO)

Account Handler
Annie Gardener (TKO)

Client/manufacturer
AXB Co Ltd

Design Group
TKO Product Design
1998

The blurred distinctions between design disciplines means that a freedom finally exists to experience design for manufacture with a holistic and progressive attitude, not restrained by the glass walls erected when design was based on the object rather that the space it occupied. Out there are companies and individuals whose cleverness and collaborative creativity sometimes results in truly new solutions.

Still, there is a never-ending push for progress which is crucial to justify first world man's obsession with the new or shiny and the demand for resources without restraint. Designers have a responsibility (usually on behalf of their clients, but also for themselves) to continuously re-evaluate what they are creating to ensure a product can justify its existence based on some kind of need rather than only because it can exist. There always seems to be a negative side to things that feel good, and the uplifting, energising and emotional trip possible (outside of love and drugs) from designing good products, casts its shadow in the consequences of constant creation, and the impact on our planet.

A cross-cultural, multidisciplinary, cross-pollination of energy and ideas is where the progressive future lies, and I intend TKO to follow that course in a kind of flexible, organic way: in many ways the original impetus for TKO's existence was based on this ideal. But however, and from wherever the creative stuff comes, you shouldn't mess with it, as it is elusive when lost. It's important then that TKO does not reflect just my personality because it's the other people – especially my business partner, Annie Gardener – who make the team what it is.

Technology itself can continue to be an enabling, empowering tool for everyone, so long as there are designers involved who have the skills to make connections between people, their desires and their circumstances, and the understanding to design because we need to, not just because we can.

Timers

Domestic Digital Timers

Design
Andy Davey, Rochelle Smith

Client/manufacturer
LEC Inc (Japan)
1998

Sub

Portable CD Player/Tuner

Design
Andy Davey (TKO),
Mashahiro Nagakubo,
Atsushi Suzuki
(Sony Corporation
Audio Design Goup)

Account Handler
Annie Gardener (TKO)

Client
Sony Corporation
Audio Design Group

Design Group
TKO Product Design
1991

Freeplay

Clockwork Radio

Design
Andy Davey (TKO)

Inventor
Trevor Baylis (BayGen)

Account Handler
Annie Gardener (TKO)

Manufacturer
BayGen Power
International Ltd

Design Group
TKO Product Design
1995/6

viemeister

**Nickelodeon Computer
Accessories**

Design
Tucker Viemeister,
Scott Henderson,
Jarrod Linton,
Stuart Harvey Lee

Design Group
Smart Design with Altitude

Client/manufacturer
Brainworks
1996

By making computer
peripherals more fun,
Brainworks intended to help
"little brains work better".
The Nickelodeon keyboards
feature a clear base to allow
inspection of the electronic
workings, the hoses serve as
handles and the extra blinking
LED's have no rhyme or
reason! The clear mouse has a
studded rubber cover to
exercise the fingers. Although
the product was designed for
kids, keyboard and mouse are
professional quality hardware.

Tucker Viemeister

Tucker Viemeister

Photograph Peter Moss

Smart Design Space

Design
Davin Stowell, Tucker
Viemeister, Tom Dair,
Risa Honig, Bryce Sanders,
Tam Thomsen, Tim Kennedy

Client
Smart Design
1996

Smart move! The new work paradigm says that people are more productive working together, than alone in their personal offices. The idea is to build ways of organising, working and storing that reflect the way in which the brain organises information: flexible, chaotic, comfortable and creative. All of the key community spaces are located along the central axis. Along the window stretches a serpentine line of personal home spaces.

Our Library

Design
Tucker Viemeister,
Henry Myerberg,
Karen Davidoff,
Gregory Hom

Design Group
frogdesign and HMA

Client
Robin Hood Foundation and Beginning with Children School
1999

A pro bono interior design and graphics project for a disadvantaged public elementary school. Without adding extra cost – but using only imagination, clever specifications, and donated goods, services and artwork – a wonderful environment for reading and writing flowers in Brooklyn, New York.

Designers shape the world. We give form to our ideas. The design of my environment not only reflects a philosophy, it determines the behaviour of people in it. The trick today is that the way we live is changing faster than our physical spaces – luckily new technology is going so fast maybe it will meet us back where we wanted to be (or should be). In the Stone Age people spent less percentage of their time "working": gathering food and building shelter than we do today. New technology could transform work back into an integral, natural family activity. I hope the new technology will allow invisible virtual work to help us return to a more relaxed pace, and help us connect with teams that are near or far.

A few years ago when Smart Design moved into its new quarters, we used the architecture and the furnishings to support (or at least express) our new way of working. Personal computers that transformed our workstations in the 80s won't be there in the next decade. So the most we can do is build offices that are flexible – tables with wheels are more than a metaphor. But the real challenge is not physical, it is designing behaviour that will help teams work better. New kinds of ethics and morals have to develop to cope with a new culture where anything goes – and too much does.

Today we are moving from the Age of Engineering to the Age of Design – we are shifting from using technology to overcome our physical problems, to being able to transform things to express our desires. When anything goes, what do we want? Design should not be something special – it should be normal. The process is what separates man from animals. It's natural to try to make things better – the problem is: "What is better?"

The problem most Americans face today is having everything we want. We are beginning to wonder what to do with it all. Storage is one of the fastest-growing consumer categories – boxes, shelves, mini-storage. At the same time garbage disposal is hitting the limits of landfill.

Sardine Light

Design
Tucker Viemeister,
Lisa Krohn

Manufacturer
Gallery 91

Client
Seibu
1988

The Sardine Light combines zoomorphic forms and utility materials into a nice snack for a cat. A metal spring forms the body of the lamp, the head is a fibreglass/polyester shade covering a bullet-shaped candelabra bulb. You aim the light by adjusting the fulcrum or weight. Design can serve a literary function, better than books because design speaks a universal language – real things. On the one hand the Sardine's dumb silhouette is a cartoon, yet the fish is an ageless religious and sexual symbol.

Joe Boxer

Watches and Packages

Design
Tucker Viemeister, Debbie Hahn, Stephanie Kim,
Paul Hamburger, Nicholas Graham

Design Group
Smart Design

Client
Timex
1995

Wearers of Joe Boxer watches aren't constantly reminded of the dreary passage of time. Instead they are gently egged on to crack a smile with any of the 100 designs, some with numbers replaced by witty words or nutty illustrations. Happy faces spin around, hands go backwards, secret messages appear with Indiglo technology or cases are filled with water and floating things. Timex licensed Joe Boxer in order to leverage the underwear brand's goofball humour. The line is a huge commercial success and the simple cylinder packages have won many design prizes.

But we have an even bigger dilemma: for the first time in the history of humanity it is possible to create anything we want – now, like President Clinton, we have to define what "it" is. Nanobots, foglets, self-organising systems, and artificial intelligence are real opportunities of the convergence of hardware and software. For the first part of human history we were in a battle for survival; since the Renaissance, we have made a major impact on our environment. The Industrial Revolution levelled the field: "form followed function". Practical function and ergonomics are basic criteria for any product. In the 70s, frog founder Hartmut Esslinger reframed it: "Form follows emotion". Robots, smart materials, intelligent appliances, *Star Trek* stuff and the World Wide Web are changing the way we design. Form is no longer constrained by materials or processes – it need only follow desire. *Hitchhiker* author Douglas Adams said, "Use the limits while we still have some." Now anything can be anything. Look at the Web where virtual environments can be like a dream. Form follows anything. We no longer have any limits. The real world will have no constraints either. This is a huge opportunity for design. Design will police these ethical issues of social strategy. This a special time for design because the new media craze is transforming the way we perceive everything – in the new world everything is interactive and experiential.

The classic design process is applicable to any changing world. My dad was an industrial designer. He made paintings and sculpture, played the piano, designed products, packaging, exhibits, homes, museums, cosmetics, jewellery, gingerbread houses, and cars. He helped design the Tucker car. Being named after a product, it seemed only natural for me to become a designer. What other occupation afforded such various challenges and was so much fun? As I grew up, it seemed as if he was playing around as much as I was. So it never occurred to me that there could be something else better to do.

Metropolitan Toaster

Made Into a Lamp

Design
Tucker Viemeister, Tom Dair,
(lamp designer unknown)

Design Group
Smart Design

Client/manufacturer
Black & Decker
1991

I found this lamp amalgamation in a lower East Side "gallery" for $75. It's made from the soft form of the Metropolitan toaster that broke the mould of Black & Decker's corporate style. Used as a lamp or a cooking appliance, it makes a friendly addition to the kitchen. Since the toaster is built around the same mechanical chassis as the number one selling unit, the styling alone allowed it to tie the sales quantities – virtually doubling Black & Decker's income!

Good Grips

Vegetable Peeler

Design
Davin Stowell, Stephen Russak Stephen Allendorf, Michael Calahan, Dan Formosa

Design Group
Smart Design

Client/manufacturer
Oxo International
1991

Oxo Good Grips kitchen gadgets, now an icon, were the first popular demonstration of the Universal Design principle. Good Grips are kitchen tools with a special transgenerational handle designed to be easy for everyone to hold. Larger in diameter for easy grip and comfort, the patented finned soft spots almost feel like the handle is holding you. They have transformed the housewares industry, won major recognition and are in the permanent collections of the National Design Museum and the Museum of Modern Art.

Tea Steeper

Design
Tucker Viemeister,
Scott Henderson

Design Group
Smart Design

Client/manufacturer
Cuisinart
1996

Rather than the austerity of geometrical forms, customers feel strong attraction to warm and organic forms. The forms create meaningful psychonomic connections to features such as allowing users to watch the tea perk up through the frosted dome.

Aero

Hairdryer

Design
Tucker Viemeister,
David Peschel

Design Group
Smart Design

Client
Remington
1995

The organic, aerodynamic styling moves towards a new definition of "modern" that is softer and more friendly. The ergonomic angle of the handle reduces wrist deflection when you point the dryer at your head. Aero is in the permanent collection of the Cooper-Hewitt National Design Museum.

 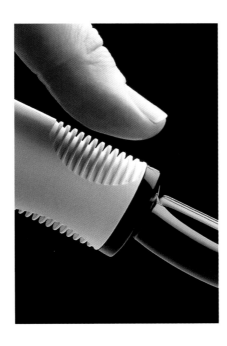  

What makes design more than a game is that it is an artistic activity that needs the social context to define it. Good design is a team effort. Not only am I making things that other people need, I work with lots of talented designers, and I also learn from my business partners. Tibor Kalman taught me that it's always best to work with people who are smarter than you are. Good clients are mediums for the designer's artistic expression.

I have three big projects. First, to encourage the convergence of hardware and software, foster multi-disciplinary teamwork, and build a smart team to create divergent products. I'm tired of little electronic gadgets with a screen pasted on the front. Soon enough the technology will fade into the walls and then designers will need to give distinction to the process – give it a physical presence. Second, I want to re-make New York as the design capital of the world. I've been trying to revitalise the design community through my work with the Industrial Design Society of America (IDSA) and the museums, schools and the consultants. Bringing atoms and bytes together is easy in New York where new media is redefining the financial and art worlds. Third, I'm also working on a couple of books. One is about my dad and the other is about Rowena Reed Kostello, my teacher at Pratt and one of the founders of the industrial design education program in the US.

Industrial design is the perfect occupation to bridge the gap from our nostalgic industrial past to the free-for-all future. We have the talent and the inclusive process to edit our options. As hardware and software converge, the designer's role must diverge. We have to use this opportunity to redefine our role in society and business. Designers combine the roles of visionary and practitioner. We can visualise the big picture because we have a grounding in the details. Designers are "objective" two ways – we have a detached perspective *and* we make objects.

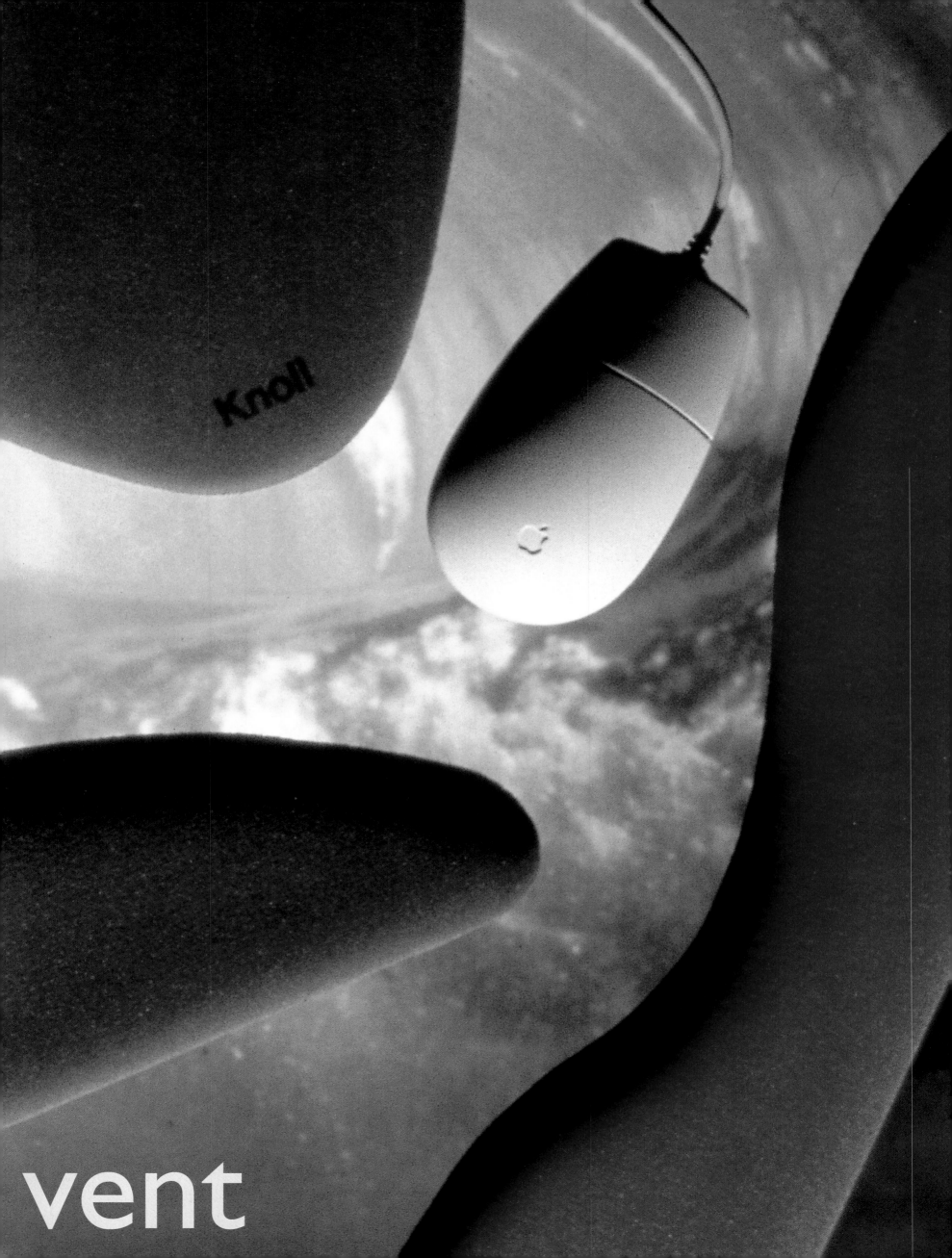

vent

Vent Design
Steve Peart

Keyboard

Design
Stephen Peart
Ross Lovegrove

Client
Knoll
1994

Adjustable Keyboard

Design
Stephen Peart

Client
Apple Computer Inc
1993

Albert Einstein once said, "Your imagination is a preview of life's coming attractions." I built a career from actualising these imaginations. In the wonderful profession that someone had the misfortune to label "industrial or product design" – good grief! ("Do you design factories? Sometimes it's easier to respond with a "yes"!) Somewhere in the following conversation the words, "art", "business" and "science" occur.

My team of four has 4000 square feet (it's not metric here yet) light industrial space, with a 20 foot headspace that has contained vertical-takeoff aircraft, pools for testing wetsuits and experimental office environments. We use and abuse computers, models and cameras for concepting and ideation of objects and scenarios to enable companies and sometimes individuals to manufacture useful stuff to get us through life. Maintaining independence – being what you call a "consultant" – is very important to providing the quality of our results. (A popular T-shirt in this Silicon Valley of four million folks reads, "I'm not unemployed, I'm a Consultant!")

I can't tell you all my secrets here but after ten years my approach involves balance awareness and horizons. Physical location with the constant improvement in aircraft, airports and communication is part of the attraction of this place, along with the required mindset. Friends who work in Hawaii complain of alien abduction – like lapses of time. This of course is too much 'mindset'. Ten hours to London, 12 to Hong Kong – whether you like it or not the world is a small place and such speeds will half in another 15 years. Which brings up one of my major peeves: it's not nukes that will get us – short-term thinking is much more of a serious threat.

Out on the Californian edge of the western culture my week often begins with someone I worked with several years ago in a totally unrelated field calling me: "It was the New Year and we decided to start a new company!" After getting off the phone from London where everyone's ready for dinner or the pub there's always a minute where you start thinking about the planet turning and that yes on the other side of the ball you guys are upside down! Watching how things exist and having the focus to evaluate is a payoff with this occupation. You get the chance to see how the world operates.

Dri Projector

Design
Stephen Peart

Client
Digital Reflection Inc
1996

Animal Surfsuit

Hi Flex System

Design
Stephen Peart

Client
O'Neill
1990

Persona

Design
Stephen Peart

Client
Sun Microsystems Inc
1998

British-born in Durham, I began my career in Germany, working for frogdesign. When the company was awarded the Apple account in 1982, I was one of four sent to start up frog's American office. Working on the ground floor of personal computing gave me an early and thorough understanding of the technical future, one I helped to mould. I was instrumental in designing many of Apple's early triumphs, most notably the ImageWriter II. Since 1987, when I founded my Campbell, CA-company, Vent, I have continued to try to describe a responsible future, but in areas that transcend the computer world.

Skateboards and wetsuits may sound like insignificant products but I was challenged to get my mind into something, to transform it into something better. The Animal wetsuit that Vent designed for O'Neill in 1990 is still the most advanced product in its class. In addition to the bold fashion statement it made to the surfing world, it drastically increased the flexibility of the user without compromising its insular functions. I also patented the new moulding system from which the suit was designed. I was not encouraged to pursue research ideas for Nike during my five years at frog: I continue in sports work investigating snowboard improvements and image studies. Bicycles also crop up from time to time.

Staying with a surfing theme, I designed several accessories in the "Surf Collection" for The Knoll Group, a New York furniture maker. In objects like the Surfboard, which is a corner device used to increase desk space, as well as a mousepad, footrest and lumbar seat support, we rendered various types of rubber, even Neoprene,

into functional biomorphic shapes. All of the projects in the Surf Collection conspire to soften the edges of the office environment.

I have not abandoned my roots in personal computers. Two of the most notable past projects – the Kensington trackable, which reduced moving parts in the objects to three, and the Apple Adjustable Keyboard, which increased the comfort of typing by splitting the keyboard in the middle, enlarging the spacebar and adding movable wristrests – have been high-profile designs. The keyboard and the Animal suit are in the New York Museum of Modern Art permanent collection – and I'm not dead yet.

Other, as they say, "high-tech" projects include the hardware that encased Java, Sun Microsystem's programming language software. From 1990–94 I was lucky to be invited onto the original "skunk" team to do hardware concepts as they were writing the software – this was mind candy for the programmers! Then there was a computer resolution wee-bam reflective chip video projector for Digital Reflection Inc that can be utilised for photographic-like TVs (using my experience, while I was with frog, of working with Sony in Japan in the 1980s where I had the small task of defining the new look strategy for Sony world TV's...); a scanner for Visioneer that scans document input in realtime; three separate video telephone models; and, a vertical wall-mounted computer for GE Plastics that allows users to constantly upgrade their CPU's without having to buy a new computer.

**100 Years into
the Future**

The Perfect Running Shoe

Design

Stephen Peart

Client

New York Times Magazine
1996

Phone in Your Ear

Design

Stephen Peart

Client

Plantronics Inc
1993

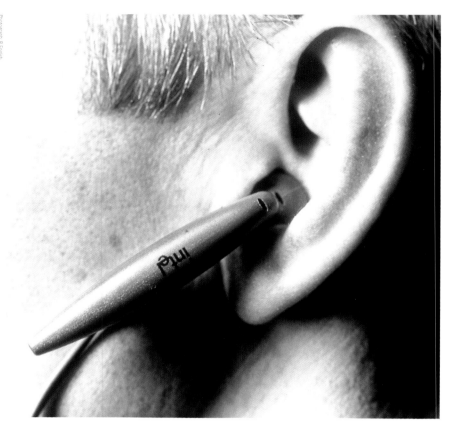

But perhaps Vent's most imaginative project in the pipeline is the new work environment for Herman Miller in Michigan. Already a few years underway, it is a collaborative work with London-based Lovegrove. An experimental "floor system" defines a new category of tools to help us in this thing we still refer to as "work". This environment is intended for new market areas: telecommuting as well as growing/shrinking small and large company structures. It draws on all aspects of my past and it's going to be fun.

We live in an age of specialisation. There are thread stores and small-breed dog walkers, and yet, somehow, I remain a confirmed generalist. This enables me to keep the big picture in focus. Look beyond the given truths of a particular field, and perhaps see a better way to design for it. We have developed a cross-fertilisation of ideas that has been extremely educational and beneficial from a design standpoint. Many of our clients get stuck. They assume their options are fixed, and my job is to find a way around those assumptions.

Many of my clients are small start-up companies that need outside help to get their businesses off the ground, but the companies most in need of consultation are large corporations. Often, "the bigger the company is, the less it can see." The irony is that the most successful, which took so many risks to start their businesses, can no longer afford to take risks... this is where design becomes invaluable.

Vent's projects may seem disparate, but they are linked by human interaction. I have a technical mind, but I'm not a technophile... I like the touchy-feely part of technology, but Humans should always be the goal.

Virtual Vision
Computer Cap

Design
Stephen Peart
Client
Virtual Vision
1996

Contributors' Biographies

These biographies relate to the individuals representing each of the design practices included in the book. As far as possible, we have included contact numbers and any further sources of information.

Apple Computer Inc

Jonathan Ive was born in 1967 in Britain and studied design at Newcastle Polytechnic. Ive is the Vice President of Design at Apple Computer Inc. Since March 1992, he has been instrumental in building and leading a design organisation that is considered one of the world's best. Prior to joining Apple in 1992, Ive was a partner in the London-based design group tangerine which he helped bring to international prominence, amassing clients that included some of the largest manufacturing corporations and most sophisticated users of design in Europe, North America, Japan and Korea. As the Apple account director at tangerine he produced a range of design studies in 1991 contributing to the PowerBook development. Ive's broad-ranging work, including the design of ceramics, televisions, VCRs and pens has been widely exhibited and published. It has been shown at design centres and museums of modern art throughout the US, Europe and Asia, receiving many awards.

Apple Computer Inc
Tel: + 1 408 996 1010 (USA)
URL: www.apple.com

Further reading

"iMac Design: The Birth of the New", *Axis*, 1999. "Apple Design: The Work of the Apple Industrial Design Group", *Graphis Inc.*, 1997.

Bergne: design for manufacture

Sebastian Bergne was born in Teheran in 1966. He studied industrial design graduating from the Central Saint Martins School of Art & Design in 1988 and the Royal College of Art in 1990. He established Bergne: design for manufacture in 1990 and is collaborating with international manufacturing companies such as Authentics, Cassina, Driade, Oluce, Wireworks, WMF and Vitra on projects from small objects to furniture for mass production. There are currently over 50 products designed by Bergne in mass manufacture. His work has been widely published, by museums such as the Museum of Modern Art, New York and the Design Museum, London and honoured with numerous international design prizes. Most recently his Lamp Shade I was chosen to be included in the permanent collection of the Museum of Modern Art in New York and he received Design Plus 99 awards for his Leg Over stool and Torso lamp manufactured by Authentics.

Bergne: design for manufacture
Tel: + 44 171 622 3333 (UK)

Further reading

Morrison, Jasper (editor), *International Design Yearbook*, Laurence King, 1999. **Levi**, Peta (general editor), *New British Design*, Mitchel Beazley, 1998. **Byars**, Mel, *50 Products*, RotoVision, 1998. **Starck**, Philippe (editor), *International Design Yearbook*, Laurence King, 1997. **Jones**, Jonathan, "Sebastian Bergne", *Modern Painters*, issue Winter 1998, p.1. **Redhead**, David, "Sebastian Bergne", *Interieur Kortik Biennale* catalogue, Interieur Foundation, pp.26–29, 76. **Azumi**, Shin, "Sebastian Bergne", *Design News Japan*, issue 242, 1998, p.102. **Romanelli**, Marco, "Sebastian Bergne – Young Inventions", *Abitare*, issue 375, 1998, p.182–187. See also issues 350, 357, 366 and 372. **Rawsthorn**, Alice, "The I.D. Forty", *I.D.* magazine issue Jan/Feb 1998, p.61. **Tasma Anargyros**, Sophie, "Sebsastian Bergne – Simple is Not Easy", *Design Report*, issue 5, 1996, pp.34–38. **Swab**, Petra, "Sebastian Bergne", *Intramuros*, issue April/May, 1997, cover and pp.28–33.

Donegani & Lauda

Dante Donegani was born in Italy in 1957 and graduated from the Faculty of Architecture in Florence in 1983. From 1987–1990 he worked at Corporate Identity Olivetti. Since 1993 he has been the Director of the Design Master Course held at Domus Academy. As well as interior design projects for private homes, stores and expositions, he has designed products for several companies including Memphis, Stildomus, Isuzu and Luceplan. His work has been exhibited across Italy and in Japan and France and has won several major awards including Manhattan Waterfront, New York, 1988 (first prize) and Berlin Wall, Berlin, 1987 (first prize) both in collaboration with A Branzi. Giovanni Lauda was born in Italy in 1956 and has a degree in architecture. Since 1988 he has lived and worked in Milan, in the field of interior, exhibition and industrial design for companies such as Artas, Play Line, Sedie & Company. From 1989 until 1992 he was a member of Morozzi & Partners design office, working on product design and corporate identity, collaborating with numerous companies among which were Edra, Formica, Ideal Standard, Mitsubishi, Nissan and Uchino. Since 1994 he has been responsible for the Design Culture course in the Industrial Design Master Course at the Domus Academy. He has collaborated with many Italian and foreign magazines writing on architecture and design. In addition, he has co-curated exhibitions such as "Il design Italiano dal 1964 al 1990", which was held at the Triennale of Milan in 1996. The company Donegani & Lauda was established in 1993 and offers many design services from exhibition design, to products for the home and office.

Donegani & Lauda
Tel: + 39 2 480 22085 (Italy)

Further reading

Bellati, Nally, *New Italian Design*, Rizzoli, 1990. **Branzi,** Andrea, *Il Design Italiano 1964–1990*, Electa, 1996. **Gili Galfetti**, Gustau, *Model Apartments*, Editorial Gustavo Gili, 1997. **Mastropietro**, Mario (editor), *Nuovo Allestimento Italiano*, edizioni Lybra Immagine, 1997. **Starck**, Philippe (editor), *International Design Yearbook 1997*, Laurence King, 1997. **Sanpietro**, Silvio (editor), *Nuovi Negozi in Italia*, Edizioni l'Archivolto, 1997. Collection, *Formes de Metropoles: Nouveaux Design in Europe*, Centres George Pompidou, 1991. **Briatore,** Virginio, "The Kitchen That Will Come", *Interni Annual Cucine*, 1998. **Donegani,** Dante and Lauda, Giovanni, "Azioni a Scomparas", *Ottagono* 122 marzo-maggio 1997, pp.56–57. **Hoger,** Hans, "Surveying The City System", *Domus* issue 809, 1998, pp.88–95.

Dyson Appliances Ltd

James Dyson was born in Norfolk in 1947 and trained at the Byam Shaw School of drawing and painting, London and the Royal College of Art where he studied furniture design then interior design. After graduating in 1970 he joined Rotork in Bath where he was appointed director in 1973. From 1974–78 Dyson struck out on his own designing a number of inventions including the Ballbarrow, the Waterolla and the Trolleyball. In 1978 he stumbled across the idea of a bagless cleaner while renovating his country house in the Cotswolds and spent the next five years developing a new vacuum cleaner, building 5,127 prototypes of the Dual Cyclone™ before launching the G-Force in 1983. Facing reluctance on the part of multinationals to licence the product, he eventually took it to Japan where it won the International Design Fair prize in 1991. With royalties from Japan, America and Canada, he was able to set up in the UK where Dyson is now the brand leader in the UK floorcare market. Dyson employs over 1,300 people, of whom 20% are design engineers working on research and development. The company has won numerous design prizes including the 1997 European Design Prize for a Young Technology Intensive Award, the 1997 Japan Industrial Design Promotion Organisation Gold Award, the 1997 European Design Prize for a Young Technology Intensive Company, the 1996 DBA Design Effectiveness Grand Prix Trophy and the 1996 ID Award.

Dyson Appliances Ltd
Tel: + 44 1666 827 200 (UK)
URL: www.dyson.com

Further reading

Dyson, James, *Against The Odds – James Dyson, An Autobiography*, Orion Business, 1998.

frogdesign

frogdesign's first office was opened in California in 1982. The company began its life as Esslinger Design, founded by Hartmut Esslinger in 1969, but was renamed at the time that the, now legendary, partnership was being forged with Apple – and in recognition of the team-driven creativity that the company stood for. Each project that frogdesign undertakes has a frogteam attached to it, and each frogteam is unique. frogteams are not about any one single person or any one specific talent. They are of no predetermined size or make-up. They are flexible, constantly changing aggregates of frog's ethos that reflect both their internal growth and external (e.g. client) needs. Almost from the beginning, frog's founders realised that the complexity of design projects was growing, even as the time available to accomplish them was shrinking. Teamwork was not a luxury but a creative necessity, a way of accelerating individual efforts and a way of co-ordinating various urgent efforts across the spectrum of a project. During frog's history, frogteams have evolved from being a group of industrial designers with global backgrounds to being a truly interdisciplinary mix of design, engineering, branding and media talents. While other companies celebrate the egos of their star creators, frog has shown that inspiration is everywhere. If you want specific names for a project, frog would have to give you a complete employee list. At frog, everyone has a stake in a project's success – and that fact is the genesis of the frogteam approach.

frogdesign
Tel: + 1 408 734 5800 (USA)
Tel: + 49 211 3020 340 (Germany)
URL: www.frogdesign.com

Further reading

Aldersey-Williams, Hugh, *New American Design: Products and Graphics for a Post-industrial Age*, Rizzoli, 1988, pp.90–95. **Hamilton**, Joan O.C., "Rebel With A Cause: How Hartmut Esslinger is Shaking Up the World of Industrial Design", *Business Week*, 3 Dec 1990, p.130–135. **Brandes**, Uta, *Hartmut Esslinger & frogdesign*, Steidl, 1992. **Yee**, Roger, "Kissed by a frog", *Contract Design*, June 1996, pp.36–39. "The Form Debate: Learning from America", *form*, issue 154/155, 1996, pp.44–51. **Esslinger**, Hartmut, "My American Dream", *form*, issue 154/155, 1996, pp.68–73. **Bertsch**, Georg-Christof, "frogdesign: Projects and Products", *Domus*, issue 782, May 1996. "The Macintosh Reborn", *Macworld*, Sept 1996, pp.104–116. *rana#1* © 1994, *rana#2* © 1996, published occasionally by frogdesign.

GK Design Group

Kenji Ekuan was born in Tokyo in 1929 and graduated from the Tokyo National University of Fine Arts and Music in 1955 and the Art Center College of Design (USA) in 1957. He established GK Industrial Design Associates in 1957 and took office as President. Ekuan was elected President of the Japan Industrial Designers' Association (JIDA) in 1970 and President of the International Council of Societies of Industrial Design (ICSID) in 1976. Since then he has chaired and directed numerous committees and festivals and is Chairman of Design for the World, Board Member of the Japan Design Foundation and Japan Society for Future Research, Visiting Professor of the Tokyo National University of Fine Arts and Music, Trustee of the Art Center College of Design (USA) and Advisory Member of University of Industrial Arts, Helsinki (Finland). Ekuan has received many awards and honours during his career including ICSID Colin King Grand Prix (1979), Honorary Membership of IDIA (Australia, 1981), International Design Award (Japan Design Foundation, 1987), World Design Award (IDSA, USA, 1988), the Blue Ribbon Medal (Japan, 1992), Sir Misha Black Medal (UK, 1995) and Officier de l'Ordre des Arts et des Lettres (France, 1997).

GK Design Group
Tel: + 813 3950 1221 (Japan)
URL: www.gk-design.co.jp

Further reading

Industrial Design (the world of Dogu, its origins, its future), Nippon Hoso Shuppan Kyokai (NHK Books), Tokyo, 1971. *The History of Kitchen Utensils*, Shibata Shoten Co, Tokyo, 1976. *Makunouchi Bento no Bigaku (the aesthetics of the Makunouchi Lunch Box)*, Goma Shobo Publishing Co, 1980. *Butsudan to Jidosha (the Buddhist altar and the automobile)*, Kosei Shuppan, Tokyo, 1986. *Material Things and Japanese*, Tokyo Shoseki, Tokyo, 1994. *Soul and Material Things*, Holp Shuppan Publishers, Tokyo 1997. *The Aesthetics of the Japanese Lunchbox*, MIT Press, 1998.

Hollington

Geoff Hollington was born in 1949. He studied at Central Saint Martins School of Art & Design, graduating in 1971 with a BA in Industrial Design (Engineering), and gained an MA in Environmental Design from the Royal College of Art in 1974. From 1976 until 1978 he worked on the design team at the new city of Milton Keynes, then in 1978 formed a consulting partnership with architect Michael Glickman. He founded Hollington, the design firm, in 1980. Several products designed by Hollington have won international awards and are in museum collections. In addition to his design work, he occasionally teaches and lectures and has written extensively for magazines including *Blueprint* and *Design*. Hollington is a Fellow of the Royal Society of Arts, International Member of the Industrial Design Society of America and Fellow of the Chartered Society of Designers.

Hollington
Tel: + 44 171 739 3501 (UK)
URL: www.hollington.com

Further reading

Aldersey-Williams, Hugh, *Hollington Industrial Design*, Phaidon Press 1990.

IDEO

Bill Moggridge was born in 1943 and studied industrial design at the Central Saint Martins School of Art & Design graduating in 1965. He was then awarded a research fellowship in Typography and Electronic Communications at Hornsey School of Art. Moggridge founded Moggridge Associates in London in 1969. In 1979 he added a second office in San Francisco to help Silicon Valley companies, as the electronics industry moved from chips to products. In 1980 he designed the first laptop computer, the GRiD Compass. During the next few years he pioneered user interface design as a discipline to be an integrated part of product development, and coined the name Interaction Design. He merged his company with David Kelley Design to form IDEO in 1991. The company now has 350 employees in ten offices around the world, including industrial designers, ergonomists, interaction designers, mechanical and electrical engineers, and model-makers. In 1993 Moggridge was appointed Visiting Professor in Interaction Design at the Royal College of Art. IDEO was recognised as Design Group of the Year at the Design Zentrum, Essen in 1996. A Principal of IDEO, Moggridge is dedicated to the user-centred design of products, services and environments, working with clients such as Canon, NEC and Steelcase. Moggridge has been active in design education throughout his career, at the Royal College of Art and the London Business School in Britain, and Stanford University in California.

IDEO
Tel:+ 1 650 688 3400 (USA)
Tel:+ 44 171 485 1170 (UK)
URL: www.ideo.com

Further reading

"Watching the Wireless", *Blueprint*, Feb 1998. "Tomorrow's World", *Creative Review*, March 1998. "IDEO Lands Top Prize in Design Week Awards", *Design Week*, 6 March 1998. "My Own Private IDEO", *Design Week*, 13 March 1998. "Novita en Produzione", *Interni*, April 1998. "Coming Soon: Radio with Pictures", *Financial Times*, May 1998. "Sistema per l'Offico", *Domus*, June 1998. "Nomad's Land", *Director*, Aug 1998. "The New British Mailboxes", *Domus*, Sept 1998. "Work of Ages", *FX*, Oct 1998. "Think Big, Act Small", *Eciffo*, Oct 1998, Japan. "18 Views on the Definition of Design Management", *Design Management Journal*, Summer 1998. "Staying in Touch", *The Wall Street Journal*, 16 Nov 1998.

JAM Design & Communications Ltd

Jamie Anley was born in Jamaica in 1972 and studied at the Bartlett School of Architecture, graduating in 1995. Astrid Zala was born in Germany in 1968 and studied fine art at Wimbledon School of Art and Goldsmith's College, graduating in 1991. In 1995 they established JAM – a design and communications agency that explores the potential of existing technology and materials as the starting point for collaborative projects. JAM teams up with leading manufacturers such as Whirlpool, Zotefoams, SGB Youngman and Philips to develop designs that communicate the excitement and innovation that is today's changing technology. Other clients include Absolut, Breitling Watches, Evian and Sony UK. Based in London's King's Cross area, JAM's portfolio is wide-ranging: from bar stools, to portable architecture, interiors and short term urban housing solutions. JAM's off-the-wall approach to design and business has brought them to the forefront of experimental and cultural design activity. Their work has been exhibited to wide acclaim in Europe, USA and Japan.

JAM Design & Communications Ltd
Tel: + 44 171 278 5567 (UK)

Further reading

McDermott, Catherine, *Twentieth Century Design*, Design Museum, Carlton, 1997. **Levi**, Peta (general editor), *New British Design 1998*, Mitchell Beazley, 1998. **Merrick**, Jay, "The Toasty-Warm World of Jam", *The Independent on Saturday Magazine*, 14 February 1998, pp.28–31. **Brampton**, Sally, "There is No British Style", *Vogue*, June 1998, pp.128–147.

James Irvine Design Studio

James Irvine was born in London in 1958 and graduated from the Royal College of Art in 1984. He moved to Milan in 1984 where he was a design consultant for the Olivetti design studio until 1992, designing industrial products under the direction of Michele De Lucchi and Ettore Sottsass. In 1987, as part of a cultural exchange organised by Olivetti, Irvine spent a year at the Toshiba Design Centre in Tokyo carrying out design research for industrial products. He returned to Milan in 1988 and opened the James Irvine Design Studio. An exhibition of his work was held at the Royal College of Art, Stockholm, in 1993. From 1993 to 1998, along with running his private studio, he was a partner of Sottsass Associati Milan and was responsible for the industrial design group. Projects in his studio today include the design of the new city bus for Hannover, 100 of which are being built by Mercedes Benz, furniture designs for B&B Italia and Magis and products for tableware for alfi.

James Irvine Design Studio
Tel: + 39 02 295 34532 (Italy)

Jasper Morrison Ltd

Jasper Morrison was born in London in 1959 and studied design at Kingston Polytechnic Design School, London and the Royal College of Art. In 1984 he studied at Berlin's HdK on a scholarship. Morrison set up Office for Design in London in 1986 and his work was included in the "Documenta 8" exhibition in Kassel in 1987, for which he designed the Reuters News Centre. In 1988 he began designing products for the German door handle producer FSB, the office furniture company Vitra, and the Italian furniture producer, Cappellini. His work has received numerous awards including an Industrie Forum Top Ten Design Prize, a Nord Rhein Westfalen Design Zentrum Prize and a selection for Italy's Compasso D'Oro. His designs are in the collections of several museums throughout the world including the Museum of Modern Art in New York. In 1995 he began a consultancy with Üstra, the Hannover Transportation Authority, by designing a bus stop for the city. His office was then awarded the contract to design the new Hannover Tram for Expo 2000. The first vehicle was presented to the public in June 1997 at the Hannover Industrial Fair, and awarded the IF Transportation Design Prize and the Ecology Award. Recent projects include a chair for the Le Corbusier-designed monastery of La Tourette near Lyon; teaching at the Royal College of Art; editing the 1999 Design Year Book; and designing exhibitions for the Vitra Design Museum and the furniture for the new Tate Gallery at Bankside.

Further reading

Morrison, Jasper, *A Book of Spoons*, Imschoot Uitgevers, Gent, 1997. **Ruthenberg**, Peter and Brandes, Uta, *A New Tram for Hannover*, Gebr. Mann Verlag, Berlin, 1997. **Morrison**, Jasper, *A World without Words*, second edition, Lars Müller, Zurich, 1998. **Boyer**, Charles Arthur and Zanco, Federica, *Jasper Morrison*, Dis Voir Editions Design Monograph, 1999. **Dormer**, Peter, (Foreword). *Jasper Morrison – Design, Projects and Drawings 1981–1989*, ADT Design Files, Design & Technology Press, London, 1990. **Morrison**, Jasper, "The Unimportance of Form", *Ottagono*, March 1996. *Domus*, issue 798, Nov 1997. *I.D.* magazine, March/April 1998.

Karim Rashid Inc

Karim Rashid was born in Egypt in 1960 and brought up in England and Canada. He received a BA in Industrial Design in 1982 from Carleton University in Ottawa, Canada and pursued graduate design studies in Naples, Italy with Ettore Sottsass and Geatano Pesce. After his studies, Rashid spent a year in Milan at the Rodolfo Bonetto Studio. On his return to Canada, he worked for seven years with KAN Industrial Designers. While there, he also co-founded and designed the Babel Fashion Collection. He opened his own practice in 1991, and in 1993 he moved his industrial design studio to New York. He has designed products and furniture for clients including Idée, Issey Miyake, Umbra, Sony, Fasem, Nambé, Tommy Hilfiger, Magis, Zanotta, Octopus and Estee Lauder. Awards include the Brooklyn Museum of Art, Designer of the Year 1998 and the George Nelson Award 1999. His work has been exhibited in major museums worldwide including Museums of Modern Art (New York and San Francisco), Toronto Design Exchange, Tokyo Gas and the Groninger Museum, Holland. Rashid has taught at several colleges across the United States, Canada and Mexico and he is currently Associate Professor in Industrial Design at the University of the Arts in Philadelphia.

Karim Rashid Inc
Tel: + 1 212 929 8657 (USA)
URL: www.core77.com/karimrashid

Further reading

Cook, Cindy, "And You Thought It Was Only A Chair", *Nylon* magazine, Premier issue, April 1999, pp.128–129. "George Nelson Award", *Interiors* magazine, June 1999. **Robbins**, Mark, "On the Table", Wexner Center for the Arts, 1999, pp.64–65. **Bernstein**, Fred, "21 for the 21st", *Metropolitan Home*, March/April 1999, p74. **Hirst**, Arlene, "Take Note", *Metropolitan Home*, March/April 1999, p.33. "Der Software-Virtuose", *Architektur & Wohnen*, Feb/March 1999, pp.24, 26, 190. **Suqi**, Rima. "Radar", *Out*, issue 62, Jan 1999, p.24. **Patton**, Phil, "From Eureka to Your House", *New York Times Magazine*, 13 Dec 1998, pp.96–100. **Lavazza**, Andrea, "Design, Too, Becomes Global", *Domus* magazine, Oct 1998, pp.70–75.

Lovegrove Studio

Ross Lovegrove was born in Wales in 1958 and graduated from Manchester Polytechnic with a first class BA Honours Industrial Design in 1980 and the Royal College of Art, London in 1983. In the early 80s he worked as a designer for frogdesign in West Germany on projects such as Sony Walkmans and Apple computers. He later moved to Paris as a consultant to Knoll International, designing the Alessandri Office System. He was then invited to join the Atelier de Nimes along with Jean Nouvel and Philippe Starck. In 1988 he returned to London and worked for clients including British Airways, Airbus Industries, LucePlan, Cappellini, Driade, Apple Computers, Olympus Cameras, Tag Heuer and Herman Miller setting up Lovegrove Studio in 1990. Winner of numerous international awards, his work has been widely published and exhibited at places including the Museum of Modern Art in New York, the Guggenheim Museum in New York, Axis Centre in Japan, the Pompidou Centre in Paris and the Design Museum in London, where in 1993 he curated the first Conran Foundation Collection. Most recently, his work was shown in a solo exhibition: "Ross Lovegrove – Design" at the Danish Museum of Decorative Art in Copenhagen, in "Ross Lovegrove Objects" in Stockholm, in "Organic Dreams" at IDEE in Tokyo and in "Sensual Organic Design" at Yamagiwa Corporation in Tokyo.

Lovegrove Studio
Tel: + 44 171 229 7104 (UK)

Further reading

Bullivant, Lucy, "Ross Lovegrove, designer", *Intramouros*, Dec 1994/Jan 1995, pp.1, 35. "British Grace", *form*, 1995, pp.1, 36. "A Good Hiding", *The Magazine*, 9 April 1995. **Sudjic**, Deyan, "Old England Discovers Design", *Blueprint*, May 1995, p.117. **Pearman**, Hugh, "All You Need is Lovegrove", *The Sunday Times Magazine*, 31 March 1996. **Pasca**, Vanni, *Lighting Affinities*, Luceplan, Milan, 1996. **Pasca**, Vanni, "Sensual Organicity", *Driade Edizioni*, 1997. "Body Language", *Design Report*, 1998. "2028 – PV Gaia", *Domus*, 1998, pp.18–83. "Intérieurs portrait", *l'Architecture D'Aujourdhui*, 1997, pp.102–113. "Lovegrove", *Design Report*, October 1995, p.10. "Design-High", *Wohn Design*, Nov/Dec 1995, p.3. "English Leather", *I.D.* magazine, May/June 1996.

Lunar Design

Jeffrey Smith was born in 1953 and studied fine arts at the University of Illinois. Gerard Furbershaw was born in 1952 and studied architecture at the University of Southern California and industrial design at San Jose State University. They co-founded Lunar Design in 1984, helping to pioneer the practice of product design in the San Francisco Bay area and to make the region a hotbed of design talent. Today, Lunar comprises 40 design, engineering, and administrative professionals working at the firm's offices in Palo Alto and San Francisco. With prestigious clients such as Hewlett-Packard, Motorola, Steelcase, Cisco Systems, Pepsi, Oral-B, Sony, Microsoft, Philips Electronics and Silicon Graphics, Lunar has become one of the top award-winning design firms in the United States, creating everything from high-end computer workstations to ergonomic toothbrushes.

Lunar Design
Tel: + 1 650 326 7788 (USA)
URL: www.lunar.com

Further reading

Smith, Jeff, "Act Strategic; Be Cool", *Design Management Journal*, Winter 1999, Vol.10 No. 1, p.46. **Welles**, Edward, "How to Get Rich in America", *Inc.* magazine, April 1999, p.40.

Marc Newson Ltd

Born in Sydney, Australia, in 1963, Marc Newson spent his childhood travelling in Europe and Asia before graduating from Sydney College of Arts in 1984 having studied jewellery and sculpture. In 1987 Newson moved to Tokyo after Teruo Kurosaki, the Japanese entrepreneur, offered to put his furniture into production through his company, Idée. He stayed until 1991, when he set up a new studio in Paris and worked with manufacturing companies including Cappellini, Flos and the Pod Watch Company. He was named Designer of the Year at the Salon du Meuble in Paris in 1993. Marc Newson's work moved in a new direction in 1995, when he designed the interior of Coast restaurant in London, and in 1996 interiors of Mash & Air in Manchester and Osman in Cologne. Subsequent interior projects include Syn Studio, a Tokyo recording studio, a worldwide chain of shops for Walter van Beirendonck's W&LT brand and a retail prototype for Apple Computers. Newson's designs have been acquired for many permanent museum collections including the Museum of Modern Art in New York, the Musée des Arts Decoratifs in Paris and London's Design Museum. In 1997 a retrospective of his work was staged at Villa Noailles in France. That same year, Newson opened an office in London to establish a larger studio capable of tackling a wider range of projects. Recent commissions include furniture for B&B Italia, the interior of a private jet, a bicycle, watches for Ikepod, a torch for Flos and household products for Magis and Alessi.

Marc Newson Ltd
Tel: + 44 171 287 9388 (UK)
URL: www.marc-newson.com

Further reading
Rawsthorn, Alice, *Marc Newson*, Booth-Clibborn Editions, 1999. *Wallpaper* magazine, April 1999, pp.104–107. *Domus* magazine, Feb 1999, pp.62–63. "Distinction Design Winner", *I.D.* magazine, August 1998. *Monument*, issue 20, cover and pp.30–42. *Blueprint*, No. 120, Sept 1995, cover and pp. 12–14.

Neumeister Design

Born in Berlin in 1941, Alexander Neumeister graduated from the Hochschule für Gestaltung, Ulm, in 1968 and won a scholarship to the Tokyo University of Arts, Department of Industrial Design. He established Neumeister Design in Munich in 1970. Its main field of activities is new transportation systems, telecommunication, electronics, computer and data processing products, as well as medical equipment. Clients include Adtranz, BMW, German Aerospace, German Railways, Grundig, Hitachi, Siemens and government agencies. Together with Gudrun Neumeister he has also co-ordinated working groups on design in developing countries, organised international workshops on cultural identity and design, as well as for design of medical equipment for developing countries. From 1983 to 1987 he was board member and vice president of ICSID, the International Council for Societies for Industrial Design and is a member of the advisory board for the IF Hannover and the University of Industrial Arts, Helsinki. His work has won many international awards, among them the Brunel Award for the design of the InterCity Experimental in 1998, the 'Design Team of the Year' Award by the Design Center Essen in 1992 and the Grand Prize by the Japanese Institute of Invention and Innovation for the design of the JR-W 500 Shinkansen in 1998. Outside Germany, Neumeister Design products have been exhibited in Los Angeles, New York, Moscow, Osaka, Barcelona, Rio de Janeiro and Sao Paulo. In 1988, Alexander Neumeister together with two Brazilian partners established NCS Design Rio with design and model workshops in Rio de Janeiro.

Neumeister Design
Tel: + 49 89 210 9620 (Germany)

Further reading
"Alexander Neumeister – a monograph", *Form Verlag*, Summer 1998.

Pentagram

Robert Brunner was born in California graduating with a degree in Industrial Design from San Jose University in 1981. He worked as a designer and project manager at several high technology companies before founding Lunar Design in 1984. In 1989, Brunner accepted the position of Director of Industrial Design at Apple Computer where he founded Apple IDg, an independent internal design group responsible for providing the company with design solutions and product ideas. He became a partner in Pentagram's San Francisco office in January 1996. Formed in 1972, there are now 16 partners and over 150 staff members at Pentagram operating from subsidiary offices in San Francisco, New York, Austin and London. Each partner has his or her own area of expertise, giving the company a broad platform for its design activities, Brunner directs a team of designers, CAD specialists and model-builders in the development of new products and design strategy. Brunner's work has been widely published in North America, Europe, Asia and Australia. His product designs have won 16 IDEA Awards from the Industrial Designers Society of America and Business Week, including six Best of Category awards. His work is included in the permanent collection of the Museum of Modern Art. His client list at Pentagram includes Toshiba, Proxima, Diba, Motorola, Samsung, Silicon Graphics, Nike, Teknion, WebTV and Command Audio.

Pentagram
Tel: + 1 415 896 0499 (USA)
URL: www.pentagram.com

Further reading
Pentagram Book Five, Monacelli Press, 1999

Philips Design

Dr Stefano Marzano was born in Italy in 1950 and holds a doctorate in architecture from the Milan Polytechnic Institute. He is Managing Director of Philips Design. During the early part of his career, he worked on a wide range of assignments for several design firms. In 1978 he joined Philips Design in the Netherlands, as Design Leader for Data Systems and Telecommunication products. He returned to Italy in 1982 to direct the Philips-Ire Design Centre (Major Domestic Appliances), becoming Vice President of Corporate Industrial Design for Whirlpool International (a joint venture of Whirlpool and Philips) in 1989. He is a professor at the Domus Academy in Milan and is a member of the Academy's Strategic Board. He is also a professor at the Politecnico di Milano, faculty of Architecture. Marzano is also a member of the Advisory Board for the New Metropolis science and technology centre in Amsterdam and a board member of the Aestron Foundation in Holland.

Philips Design
Tel: + 31 40 275 9066 (Netherlands)
URL: www.design.philips.com

Further reading
Marzano, Stefano, *Creating Value By Design: Thoughts*, V+K Publishing, 1998. **Marzano**, Stefano, *Creating Value By Design: Facts*, V+K Publishing, 1998.

Priestman Goode

Paul Priestman was born in 1961 and educated at the Central Saint Martin's School of Art & Design and the Royal College of Art. Nigel Goode was born in 1960 and educated at Leicester Polytechnic and the Central School of Art. They established Priestman Goode, a London-based product design and development consultancy, in 1986. The studio comprises 15 product designers, working with village specialists as projects require. Active in a broad range of product areas, projects by Priestman Goode have won many awards including, in 1998, an IF German Industrial Design Award and three UK Millennium Products awards. Their work has also been selected for permanent display at the Philadelphia Museum of Modern Art, USA.

Priestman Goode
Tel: + 44 171 935 6665

Further reading
Redhead, David, "Profile Priestman Goode", *Blueprint*, May 1998. **Algie**, Jim, "Soft Tech", *Art 4D*, June 1998. **Prigg**, Mark, "Smallest Hi-Fi", *The Sunday Times*, June 1998.

Renault

Born in France in 1945 but educated in Great Britain, Patrick le Quément graduated from the Birmingham Institute of Art and Design in 1966. He worked briefly for Simca in France before going abroad, where he worked for 17 years at the Ford Motor Company and two years for the Volkswagen Group. In 1987 he was appointed Vice President of Design at Renault and is currently Senior Vice President in charge of Quality and Industrial Design. He was also appointed Chairman of the Board of the ENSCI (Ecole Nationale Supérieure de Création Industrielle) school in 1998. Patrick le Quément was awarded the French National Prize for Design in 1992 and is a Chevalier de la Légion d'Honneur.

Renault
Tel: + 331 4104 5522 (France)
URL: www.renault.com

Further reading

Cumberford, Robert, "The French Direction, portrait of Patrick le Quément", *Automobile* magazine, April 1998. "In the Name of Design: le Crayon de Renault", International Review, *Air France Magazine*, Oct 1998. "Blick zuruck nach Vorn revue", *Auto Focus*, Nov 1998. "Patrick le Quément: l'art de surprendre au volant, Le vif," *l'Express*, Belgium.

Ron Arad & Associates

Ron Arad was born in Tel Aviv in 1951 and studied at the Jerusalem Academy of Art before moving to London in 1973. Between 1974–79 Arad studied under Peter Cook and B Tschumi at the Architectural Association, School of Architecture. In 1981 he established One Off Ltd, a design studio, workshops and showroom in London, with Caroline Thorman. Their first success was with a range of furniture and interior sculptures in tube and cast iron fittings. Well-known pieces include the Rover Chair, the vacuum-packed Transformer Chair and the remote-controlled Aerial Light. In 1989, Ron Arad Associates, an architecture and design practice, was founded (again with Caroline Thorman) and the Ron Arad Studio was established in Como in 1994 to continue and expand on the production studio pieces previously produced in the London workshops. Ron Arad was Professor of Product Design at the Hochschule in Vienna from 1994–97, Professor of Furniture Design at the Royal College of Art (RCA), London in 1997 and is Professor of Industrial Design and Furniture Design at the RCA. He was guest editor of the 1994 International Design Yearbook and Designer of the Year and his work has been widely featured in many design/architectural books and magazines worldwide.

Ron Arad Associates
Tel: + 44 171 284 4963 (UK)

Further reading

Sudjic, Deyan, *Ron Arad*, Laurence King, 1999. Guidot, Raymond, *Ron Arad*, Olivier Boissiere, Dis Voir, 1998. Albus, Volker, *Design Classics Bookwork*, Form Verlag, 1997. Ron Arad Associates, *One Off Three*, Artemis Architectural Publications, 1993. Sudjic, Deyan, *Restless Furniture*, Fourth Estate, 1989, reprinted 1990. von Vegesack, Alexander, *Ron Arad*, Vitra, 1990.

Seymour Powell

Richard Seymour was born in 1953 and studied graphic design at the Central Saint Martin's School of Art & Design and the Royal College of Art. He worked as an art director in advertising for five years before turning to product design. Dick Powell was born in 1951 and studied industrial design at Manchester Polytechnic and the Royal College of Art. Having formed their own companies after graduating, they finally decided to pool their individual skills to form a company which could undertake product design in a new way: from the consumer's point of view rather than the slavish repackaging of existing solutions. This approach brought early success when Seymour Powell created the world's first cordless kettle in 1987, a user-focused development which has now completely overtaken the kettle industry. Since then, Seymour Powell has grown modestly in terms of size (now only 26 people), but dramatically in terms of influence and portfolio. As this book goes to press, SP has five international automotive clients and 25 other blue-chip clients in areas as diverse as wristwatches and sanitary ware. The consultancy has received numerous international awards for its design work, especially in the field of transportation design.

Seymour Powell
Tel: + 44 171 381 6433 (UK)

Starck

Philippe Starck was born in Paris in 1949 and educated at Notre Dame de Sainte Croix in Neuilly and Ecole Nissim de Camondo in Paris. He established Starck Product in 1979 and went on to become one of France's best-known designers working across a range of disciplines from product to furniture, architecture and interior design. His many clients have included the French government, Café Costes, 3 Suisses (for whom he designed a mail-order self-build house), Fluocaril, Alessi, Kartell, Cassina and Driade. From 1993–96 he was worldwide Artistic Director for Thomson Consumer Electronics. His work has won numerous international awards including three in the USA for the Royalton and Paramount Hotels in New York, Primero Internacional de Diseno Barcelona and the Harvard Excellence in Design award. In 1998 he received a Commandeur dans l'Ordre des Arts et des Lettres from the French government. He has taught at the Domus Academy, Milan and l'Ecole des Arts Décoratifs in Paris. His work has been the subject of many exhibitions in Europe, Japan and the USA. One of his most recent projects, the Good Goods catalogue with La Redoute, aims to bring high quality design to the masses.

Starck
Tel: + 33 1 41 08 82 82 (France)

Further reading

Starck, Philippe, Renaud, Philippe and Wiame, Laurent, *Philippe Starck: Mobilier 1970–1987*, Michel Aveline, 1987. Philippi, Simone (editor), *Starck*, Taschen, 1996. Sweet, Fay, *Philippe Starck: Subverchic Design*, Thames & Hudson, 1999.

StudioBrown

Born in England in 1955, Julian Brown studied industrial design at Leicester Polytechnic, later graduating from the Royal College of Art in 1983. After graduating he moved to Austria to join the Porsche Design Studio and designed the Porsche Design Studio spectacles. In 1986 he co-formed the Lovegrove and Brown studio in London and in 1990, established the independent consultancy, StudioBrown. He designs for a broad spectrum of international manufacturing companies, including Rexite Spa, alfi, Sony, Apple, Curver, NEC and Acco. His designs have won many international design awards culminating in winning Best of Category award in the consumer product section of the 1998 I.D. Magazine USA Annual Design Review with the tape dispenser Hannibal for the Italian manufacturer Rexite. Brown was a guest Professor at the Hochschule der Kuenste in Berlin in 1992, is external examiner for the postgraduate course in Industrial Design at the Royal College of Art and acts as juror on a number of design competition panels. In 1998 he was elected Royal Designer for Industry by the Royal Society of Arts in London.

StudioBrown
Tel: + 44 1225 481 735 (UK)

Further reading

Marples, Peter, "British Design", *Design World*, issue 23, 1992, pp.38–41. Evamy, Michael, "Product Design Case Study", *Design* magazine, Aug 1993, title page, pp.16–20. Ambühl, Katrin, "Recycling macht Spass", *Wohn Revue*, July 1996, pp.122–4. Evamy, Michael, "Schönes Recycling", *Design Report*, issue 9, 1996 pp.58–61. "Consumer Products", 44th Annual Design Review, *I.D.* magazine, July 1998, pp.98–99. Kürschner, Jochen H, "Gedeckter Tisch", *Porzellan und Glas*, Sept 1998, title page, p.85. Goldschmiedt, Maria Clara, "Il Faro della Gran Bretagna", *Capital*, March 1997, p.179. Corliss, Richard and Booth, Cathy, "The Best of Design", *Time*, 21 Dec 1998, p.83. Azumi, Shin, "London Creative Scene", *Design News*, Winter (244) 1998, profile 01.

Studio Sowden Design Associates

Studio Sowden was opened in Milan in 1980. Based on the work and design research of George J Sowden, the studio has developed in many directions, covering different aspects of product design, from artisan to industrial production. Three years ago the studio became Studio Sowden Design Associates, with four partners: George J Sowden, Davy Kho, Hiroshi Ono and Franco Mele. Studio Sowden Design Associates is building on the experience Studio Sowden accumulated over the last two decades and offers a range of services from design concepts, aesthetic research/styling, product engineering and 3-D information for tooling. Working for clients such as IPM, Alessi, Olivetti and Telecom Italia, the Studio has won numerous awards including the Smau Award and the Compasso d'Oro. Today all the design and engineering is created mathematically, in 3-D from Unix workstations. This enables models and prototypes to be constructed virtually with fine tolerances and complete control. The transfer of information from the Studio to CAD/CAM milling machines for the construction of physical presentation models, working samples and tooling is rapid and precise.

Studio Sowden Design Associates
Tel: +390 265 3089 (Italy)

Further reading

Brandes Erlhof, Baake, *Design als Gegenstand*, Frölich & Kauffman, 1983. **Radice**, Barbara, *Memphis*, Electa, 1984. **Collins**, Michael & Papadakis, Andreas, *Postmodern Design*, Rizzoli, 1989. *George J Sowden Designing 1970–1990*, Musée des Arts Decoratifs, Centre National des Arts Plastiques, 1990. **Annicchiarico**, Silvana, "Electronic Craftsmen", *Modo*, issue 194, Dec/Jan 98-99. **Mascheroni**, Lordeana, "The Roots of Design", *Domus*, issue 812, Feb 99.

tangerine

Martin Darbyshire was born in Britain in 1961 and studied at Central St Martin's School of Art & Design, graduating in 1983. He founded tangerine with one other partner in 1989. Over the last ten years tangerine has worked with more than fifty clients, building up a broad portfolio of work designing products for the telecommunications, electronic consumer goods, housewares, transport and healthcare sectors. Clients include British Airways, Apple Computers, Hitachi, LG Electronics, Waterford Wedgwood and Procter & Gamble. 70% of tangerine's project work comes from outside the UK, ranging from the USA, through Europe to the Far East, and to date they have won six design awards: three in the USA, two in Europe and one in Japan. They work with clients both large and small, as well as co-operating with small research groups. tangerine believe that 80% of a product's potential is defined in the early stages of the design process.

It is in these stages that important decisions are made that set not only the appearance of a product, but also its cost, longevity, environmental impact and many other factors.

tangerine
Tel: + 44 171 357 0966 (UK)
URL: www.britishdesign.co.uk

Further reading

Aldersey-Williams, Hugh, "Soul Food for Designers", *Inside Business* (Independent on Sunday), 19 April 1998, p.8. **March**, David, "Challenging Perceptions", *Industrial Design in Practice*, April 1998, p.63. **Aldersey-Williams**, Hugh, "Soul in Products", *Viewpoint*, issue 3, March 1998. **Valentine**, Matthew, "Design for Ability Research", *Design*, Spring 1997. **Johnston**, Malcolm and Barber, Jo, "Ordinary People", *Design*, Spring 1996. **Evamy**, Michael, "After the Black Box", *Blueprint*, Feb 1995, p.36.

TKO

Andy Davey was born in 1962 and educated at West Sussex College of Art and Design and the Royal College of Art. Davey is creative director and Principal of TKO Product Design, the award-winning consultancy he founded with Annie Gardener in 1990. He remains the creative force behind TKO's work and has been responsible for products that range from leading-edge consumer electronics to eyewear, lighting, appliances and toys. TKO has collaborated with manufacturing and product development companies in the UK and overseas such as Alcatel, Canon, Hasbro, Honda, Mars, NEC and Sony since its formation. From its core base in product design – with recent work ranging from professional medical products and mobile telephones to computer games peripherals and snowboards – TKO increasingly responds to clients' requirements for multi-media presentations, co-ordinated product, packaging and identity strategies, trends research and web design. TKO has won many awards including, most recently, a Special Award of the Japan Display Design Association for the Crystal Mu LCD computer display for NEC Design Ltd, Japan.

TKO
Tel: + 44 171 490 2505 (UK)
URL: www.tkodesign.co.uk

Further reading

Sapper, Richard (editor), *The International Design Yearbook* 1998, Calman & King, London, 1998. **Catterall**, Claire, "Powerhouse UK", DTI exhibition catalogue, Aspen Publishing, London, 1998. **McDermott**, Catherine, *Twentieth Century Design*, Carlton Books, London, 1997. **Conran**, Terence, *Conran on Design*, Conran Octopus, London, 1996. **Frayling**, Christopher and Catterall, Claire (editors), *Design of the Times: one hundred years of the Royal College of Art*, exhibition catalogue, London, Richard Dennis Publications, 1996.

Tucker Viemeister

Tucker Viemeister was born in Ohio in 1948 and studied industrial design at the Pratt Institute, graduating in 1974. As a child growing up in Ohio, he saw the fun his father had as an industrial designer and his mother's commitment to her social work. These influences come together in Viemeister's own design career. As a Pratt graduate (BID '74), he serves as a Founding Trustee of the Rowena Reed Kostellow Fund and teaches across the US and in France. His has received many awards for his work including the annual ID Design Review (11 times) and the IDEA awards (seven times), and his work is represented in the permanent collections of the Cooper-Hewitt and the Museum of Modern Art. In 1979, Viemeister began working with David Stowell and was a founding partner and Vice President of Smart Design Inc that they set up six years later. Their most successful products include the Oxo Good Grips universal kitchen tools, the advanced technology Serengeti sunglasses and Black & Decker's Metropolitan toaster. In 1997, Hartmut Esslinger asked him to open a frogdesign studio in New York City. *Business Week* proclaimed: "Two of the most famous and mercurial figures in the product-design world are linking up." He left frog in 1999 to join Razorfish Inc as Executive Vice President, Research and Development – bringing a new dimension of change management to the digital communications consultancy. Razorfish has eight offices in eight cities around the world (including London) and global clients to keep them all busy.

Razorfish
Tel: + 1 212 966 5960 (USA)
URL: www.razorfish.com

Further reading

Rhodes, Clair, "Probing Art and Commerce," *Surface*, No. 15, Nov 1998, p.40. **Matranga**, Victoria, *American at Home: A Celebration of Twentieth-Century Housewares*, National Housewares Manufacturers Association, pp.90, 141. **Louie**, Elaine. "Earthly Offices a frog Could Love," *New York Times*, 9 July 1998, p. F8. **Choi**, Yoon, *KIDI* magazine, No.160, 9–10, 1998, pp.114–18. **Sunakawa**, Hajime. "Design Strategy for Slow and Matured Market," *Monthly Small Business*, Aug 1998, pp.16–18.

Vent Design

Stephen Peart was born in England in 1958 and educated at the Sheffield City Polytechnic where he received a first class BA Honours Degree in Industrial Design. He then graduated from the Royal College of Art in London with a Masters Degree in Industrial Design. After starting his professional career in London, Peart went on to work for frogdesign in Germany and California as Design Director for five years. In 1987 he established his own design consultancy, Vent, in Campbell, California. Vent's client list includes Apple Computer, Nike, GE Plastics, Herman Miller, The Knoll Group, Sun Microsystems, Visioneer, COM21, Jetstream, Plantronics and O'Neill.

Vent Design
Tel: + 1 408 559 4015 (USA)

Further reading

Iovine, Julie, "Ground Zero – New Concepts for Herman Miller", *I.D.* magazine, Nov 1998, pp.80–83. **Loukin**, Andra, "New Design Concepts for Herman Miller", *Interior Design*, Sept 1998, no.11, pp.152–153. "Clip in Furniture – Herman Miller", *Blueprint*, Oct 1998. **Kunkel**, Paul, "Apple's Designs 1977–1997", *Graphis*, 1997. "Design of the Times: 100 Years of Work at The Royal College of Art", *form*, 153, Jan 1996.

Select Bibliography

Aav, Marianne & Strizler-Levine, Nina (eds), *Finnish Modern Design: Utopian Ideals and Everyday Realities, 1930–97*, Bard Graduate Centre for Studies in the Decorative Arts, 1998.

Abbott, Howard, *Safer by Design: the Management of Product Design Risks*, The Design Council, 1987.

Bogle, Michael, *Design in Australia 1880–1970*, Craftsman House, 1998.

Byars, Mel, *50 Products: Innovations in Design and Materials*, Rotovision, 1998.

Dormer, Peter, *An Illustrated Dictionary of Twentieth Century Designers*, Headline, 1991.

Flinchum, Russel, *Henry Dreyfuss: Industrial Designer: the Designer in the Brown Suit*, Cooper-Hewitt, 1997.

Glaser, Milton, *Work, Life, Tools: the Things We Use to Do the Things We Do*, Monacelli Press, 1997.

Hiesinger, Kathryn B and Marcus, George H, *Landmarks of Twentieth Century Design: An Illustrated Handbook*, Abbeville Press, c1993.

Julier, Guy, *The Thames and Hudson Encyclopaedia of Twentieth Century Design*, Thames & Hudson, 1993.

Klatt, Jo & Staeffler, Gunter, *Braun and Design Collection: 40 Jahre Braun Design 1955–1995*, Klatt Design and Design Verlag, 1995.

Kunkel, Paul, *Apple Design: the Work of the Apple Industrial Design Group*, Graphis, 1997.

Levi, Peta (editor), *New British Design*, Mitchel Beazley, 1998.

Lorenz, Christopher, *The Design Dimension: the New Competitive Weapon for Product Strategy & Global Marketing*, Blackwell, 1990.

McDermott, Catherine, *Twentieth Century Design*, Carlton, 1997.

Nicholas Grimshaw & Partners, *Fusion*, Grimshaw & Partners, 1998.

Noblet, Jocelyn de, *Design: le Geste et Compas*, Somogy, c1988.

Oakley, Mark, *Design Management: a Handbook of Issues & Methods*, Blackwell Reference, 1990.

Petroski, Henry, *Invention by Design: How Engineers Get From Thought to Thing*, Harvard University Press, 1996.

Pile, John F, *Dictionary of Twentieth Century Design*, Facts on File, c1990.

Pina, Leslie, *Furniture 2000, Modern Classics & New Designs in Production*, Schiffer, 1998.

Russell, Dale, *Colour in Industrial Design*, Design Council, c1991.

Schulman, Denis, *Le Design Industriel*, Presses Universitaires de France, 1991.

Staal, Gert & Suyling, Peik (editors), *The Valid Product: Young Designers and Industry*, De Baile, 1997.

Staal, Gert et al (editors), *Young Designers Trigger Industries Trigger Young Designers*, De Baile, 1996.

Tapiovaara, Ilmari with an introduction by Pekka Korvenmaa, *Ilmari Tapiovaara*, Santa and Cole Ediciones de Diseño, 1997.

Votolato, Gregory, *American Design in the Twentieth Century*, Manchester University Press, 1998.

Zukowsky, John (editor), *Japan 2000: Architecture and Design for the Japanese Public*, Prestch, 1998.

European Arango International Design Exhibition, *Refuse: Making the Most of What We Have*, Cultural Connections, 1997.

International Design Review 1997: Industrial, Architectural & Interior Design, Logos, 1997.

Nederlands Ontwerp 1998/1999: Grafisch, Ruimtelijk, Industrieel, BIS Publishers, 1998.

Storia del Disegno Industriale, Electa, c1989.

Catherine McDermott

Catherine McDermott is a Reader in Design History at Kingston University and a Consultant Curator at the Design Museum. She has published widely in the field of contemporary design, including *Street Style, British Design in the 80s*, a series of monographs on British designers including Ben Kelly, Terry Jones and English Eccentrics and in 1997 the Design Museum book, *Twentieth Century Design*. In addition she has curated a series of exhibitions relating to contemporary design both at home and abroad. In 1998 she was commissioned by Earl Spencer to work on an exhibition on the life of his sister, Diana, Princess of Wales which has won several awards.

Kate Stephens

Kate Stephens studied Graphic Design Communication at Brighton University. On graduating she went to work for Wolff Olins and while there devised the 3i symbol which is now recognised as a landmark in contemporary design. In 1986 Kate became an independent designer working on a broad range of design projects. She is best known for her work with British artists and galleries including The Whitechapel Art Gallery – since 1989 she has designed all the gallery's catalogues, books and posters as well as a new corporate identity. Working closely with artists has often resulted in some highly creative solutions and Kate has won several awards including two D&AD Silvers for the ABSA Annual Report for which she commissioned artists to produce a series of works. In 1998 Kate was nominated for The Rowland Hill Award for Innovation in Stamp Design for the stamp series, Henry VIII and his wives.

D&AD

British Design & Art Direction (D&AD) is a professional association and educational charity working on behalf of the design and advertising communities. Our purpose is to set creative standards, educate and inspire the next creative generation, and promote the importance of good design and advertising to the business arena.

For further information please visit our website www.dandad.org or contact

D&AD
9 Graphite Square
Vauxhall Walk
London SE11 5EE
Tel: + 44 171 840 1111
Fax: + 44 171 840 0840

191